W9-BIJ-518

Baby &
Toddler Play

GYMBOReE
PLAY & MUSIC

Baby &
Toddler Play

W
O

Gymboree
Play & Music

Produced by Weldon Owen Inc.,
415 Jackson Street, San Francisco, California 94111,
in collaboration with Gymboree Play Programs,
500 Howard Street, San Francisco, California 94105

GYMBOREE PLAY & MUSIC

Chief Executive Officer: **Matthew McCauley**
Vice President, Gymboree Play & Music: **Jill Johnston**
Merchandise Manager: **Dawn Sagorski**
Senior Program Developer: **Helene Silver Freda**

Printed in China by 1010

10 9 8 7 6 5 4 3 2 1

2011 2012 2013 2014

ISBN 978-1-61628-146-5

WELDON OWEN INC.

CEO and President: **Terry Newell**
VP and Publisher: **Roger Shaw**
VP, Sales and New Business Development: **Amy Kaneko**
Production Director: **Chris Hemesath**
Executive Editor: **Elizabeth Dougherty**
Creative Director: **Kelly Booth**
Designer: **Meghan Hildebrand**
Photographer: **Chris Shorten**
Illustrator: **Matt Graif**
Writers: **Mona Behan, Susan Elisabeth Davis,
    Christine Loomis, and Genevieve Morgan**

Acknowledgments: Rebecca Poole Forée, Brynn Breuner,
Jennifer Block Martin, Jane B. Mason, and Sarah Hines
Stephens for editorial; Colin Wheatland and Emma Forge
for art direction; and Amy Perl Photography for additional
cover photography.

SPECIAL NOTE ON SAFETY PRECAUTIONS

At Gymboree, we encourage parents to become active play partners with their children. As you enjoy these enriching activities with your child, please make safety your priority. While the risk of injury during any of these activities is low, take every precaution to ensure your child is as safe as possible.

To reduce the risk of injury, please follow these guidelines: Do not leave your child unattended, even for a brief moment, during any of the activities in this book; be particularly cautious when participating in the activities involving water because of the risk of drowning; ensure that your child does not place in his or her mouth any small objects (even those depicted in the photos) as some may pose a choking hazard and could be fatal if ingested; make sure crayons, markers, and other writing and crafts materials are nontoxic and have been approved for use by children under three years of age.

Throughout this book, we have suggested guidelines to the age-appropriateness of each activity; however, it is up to you to assess your own child's suitability for a particular activity before attempting it. Ability, balance, and dexterity vary considerably from child to child, even for children of the same age.

While we have made every effort to ensure that the information is accurate and reliable, and that the activities are safe and workable when an adult is properly supervising, we disclaim all liability for any unintended, unforeseen, or improper application of the recommendations and suggestions featured.

CONTENTS

continued on next page ➤

7

CONTENTS

TYPES OF ACTIVITIES

IMAGINATIVE PLAY

MUSIC & MOVEMENT

continued on next page ➤

TYPES OF ACTIVITIES

13

FOREWORD

CHILDREN LEARN through play, and playing with your child is one of the most important things you do as a parent. Luckily, it can also be one of the easiest and most enjoyable. As a parent, you will be your child's favorite playmate. The good news is you don't need any special training or expensive toys to be a wonderful companion and teacher. All it takes is time together with your little one.

During playtime, babies and toddlers learn about themselves, other people, and the world in which they live. Children develop physical, emotional, cognitive, and social skills through play. Simply talking or singing to your infant assures her that she's loved, improves her hearing, and teaches her social skills. With every game of peekaboo, you're teaching your child that you still exist even when you're out of sight. Understanding this gives your child the security of knowing you will come back – which, in turn, eases separation anxiety and promotes independence. Dance to music with a toddler, and he gains spatial awareness, fine-tunes gross motor skills, and feels rhythm, which lays the groundwork for literacy.

If you're a new parent looking for inspiration or if you'd like to expand your play repertoire, *Baby & Toddler Play* is a must-have resource. Based on Gymboree's highly successful *Baby Play* and *Toddler Play* activity books, *Baby & Toddler Play* is a compilation of Gymboree's best activities for parents and children, featuring more than 170 fun and educational activities. Child development experts designed the activities in the book for parents and children newborn to age 3. They conceived each activity first and foremost to be fun – skill development and learning naturally follow.

The book's first section, Baby Play, is for children from birth to 12 months. The second, Toddler Play, is for children ages 1 to 3 years old. Each section contains age-appropriate games, songs, and exercises for mind and body – from imitating facial expressions to chasing bubbles, from playing balance games to exploring the backyard from a different perspective.

The color photos of parents and children in this book serve a dual purpose. They demonstrate how to do the activities. But because kids love to look at other kids, they also entice children to interact with the book. (Don't be surprised if looking though the book itself becomes a favorite activity.)

Baby & Toddler Play will help you discover new ways to play with your child, understand how these activities help your child learn and develop, and – most important – give your family hours of fun.

PLAYING WITH YOUR BABY

WHEN YOU FIRST bring a new baby home, your thoughts are usually full of the practical matters: how to keep your baby clean, warm, and well-fed; where to store the tiny diapers and clothes; how the car seat and stroller actually work; and getting some sleep.

Once the necessities are taken care of, there's something further that even the littlest baby needs in order to thrive: warm, playful interactions with the caretakers around him. Dozens of studies in recent years have shown that a child's sense of self-

LEARNING is only part of the fun.

esteem and his ability to form close emotional ties with others greatly depends upon the quality of his bond with his parents. This bond can be enhanced by close, loving play. Indeed, for babies who cannot yet go to school or read a book, play is the primary way they learn.

THE INCREDIBLE FIRST YEAR

During the first 12 months, babies undergo a profound mental, physical, and social awakening. They learn to recognize their families, the cabinet with the crackers, and the playground with the big slide. They learn to support their heads, use their hands, roll over, sit, crawl, stand, and — in some cases — walk. And long before they are ready to speak, they understand a range of human communication, from body language (the quick head shake that discourages further food throwing) to some of the words you say. At the same time, they learn how to communicate their needs and feelings through their very own baby language.

The greatest task in the first year is the development of a baby's trust. Your baby needs to know

LEARNING to crawl creates opportunity for more adventurous play activities.

later intellectual, emotional, and physical life depends upon the kinds and amount of stimulation she receives in her earliest years.

Such talk of stimulation and mental development has a tendency to sound awfully dry. Play, however, comes naturally to most babies – and to most parents. Inspire yourself by remembering babies aren't born knowing how much fun the world can be, and you get to show them.

that his physical needs for food and warmth will be fulfilled, that his environment is safe, and, most important, that his caretakers will cherish him and nourish his own budding feelings of love. Hugging, kissing, rocking, and smiling are ways of cultivating this trust. So is introducing your baby to the simple joys of all different kinds of play.

Interacting with your child is vitally important throughout his life, of course. But in the first year play can be especially important and rewarding. Researchers estimate that 50 percent of a human's brain development occurs in the first six months of life; 70 percent is complete by the end of the first year. While much of this development has to do with genetic heritage, a good portion of a child's

ALL KINDS OF PLAY

Babies don't know right away that stuffed animals are for hugging or that peekaboo games provide riotous good fun, or that pinwheels sparkle as they spin. Bringing games and toys to your baby, along

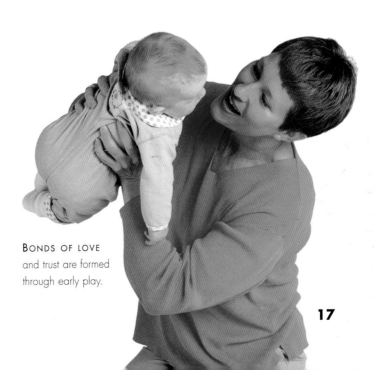

BONDS OF LOVE and trust are formed through early play.

17

with your attention, laughter, and encouragement, lets both of you share in the explorations.

Another task for parents during this first year is to tune in to their babies as individuals. Play, even "stimulating" play, isn't really about force-feeding experiences, but is rather about understanding your baby's temperament: her likes and dislikes and her tolerance for and ability to adapt to stimulation. Some babies love to be rocked back and forth, while others strongly object. Some like to be chased; others are uncomfortable with such rowdiness. Respond to your baby's cues and follow her lead.

Babies have distinct cycles of rest and activity, attention and inattention. The best time for active play – swatting at toys, rolling balls, or knocking over blocks – is when your baby is receptive and

A GOOD GAME provides lots of smiles, giggles, and future memories.

alert. Opt for more passive play – listening to songs or snuggling up with a book – when he is subdued. Both types are important. It's the timing that counts.

Spontaneity can make play even more fun and rewarding, and you'll find opportunities at every turn. Add peekaboo games to diaper changes to minimize squirming. Play "I'm gonna get you" as you're leaving the house together and you'll get out the door quicker – and in probably better humor.

Burst into song in the car and your baby's fussing may turn into giggles.

Viewed this way, play becomes less about achieving accomplishments and more about creating relationships. When you play with your baby, you're engaging in intimate activities that help him master certain skills while also creating a loving and joyful bond.

A GENTLE KISS provides the perfect end to a knee ride.

The following activities are grouped chronologically in three-month age ranges that match key stages in a baby's development. These are general guidelines only, as there is a wide range of developmental differences among children.

FROM BIRTH AND UP

At first glance, your newborn may seem unable to do much. But he is actually taking in volumes of information about his world through all his senses. In these early months he will make steady gains in his ability to control his muscles. Sometime in his second month his tightly closed fists may begin to open. Then he'll swipe at objects. Play isn't so much about lively activity as it is about sensory exploration —giving him objects to watch, listen to, and touch.

3 MONTHS AND UP

The second three months of your baby's life introduce the dawn of her sense of control over her world, however elementary. No longer a passive newborn, your baby is stronger and more active. She can now use her hands to reach out and pull objects into her world and then drop them, or put them in her mouth as a means of exploration. These activities are learning experiences through which she develops all kinds of skills along with her sense of self.

6 MONTHS AND UP

By now, your baby is a charmingly social creature, one who laughs and calls out to garner attention or provoke a response. He's also a mobile baby, one who can roll over, creep, crawl, or pull himself up to get what he wants. He will test his emerging fine motor skills by carefully bringing his thumb and forefinger together, fiddling with labels or crumbs. He's starting to understand that an object exists even when it isn't visible. Such conceptual developments make peekaboo and other hiding games possible.

9 MONTHS AND UP

At this age, even those babies who aren't yet walking are beginning to look and act like toddlers. Games that allow your baby to practice gross motor skills —crawling, pulling himself up to stand, toddling across the floor, or climbing —are particularly appealing to him now, because mobility is his main objective. Fine motor skills are equally important to him. He may insist on turning the pages of a book or stacking up a pile of his own. This is the beginning of the "do it myself" stage.

FROM BIRTH
0
AND UP

SWAYING, SWAYING

LAPS AND LULLABIES

SKILLSPOTLIGHT

The sensory stimulation
*provided by this activity – the
sound of your voice, the feel of
your hands, and the sight of your
face – can reassure and soothe
your baby. This activity may
even put her to sleep. And as
she approaches three
months, your smiles
and words may inspire
her to coo and grin
socially in return.*

Body Awareness	✓
Listening	✓
Visual Development	✓

SHE LOVES TO HEAR your voice, she loves to feel your touch, and she loves to be rocked rhythmically from side to side. You can combine all three of these soothing elements by using your lap as a cradle and your voice as a lullaby. Sit in a chair with your baby lying on your thighs, her feet pointing toward your stomach. Cradle her head with your hands and gently sway your body from side to side as you talk or sing to her.

GAZING INTO HER EYES
as you sway from side to
side – that's what builds
the deepest ties.

20

POM-POM PLAY

FROM BIRTH
0
AND UP

A TOUCH AND SIGHT GAME

BABIES AREN'T BORN knowing how to visually track an object or how objects move through space. Such developments take time. This gentle game will engage his attention, stimulate his senses, and eventually make him smile.

• Gather together some large brightly colored pom-poms or small plush toys. Get the baby's attention by holding the toy twelve to fifteen inches above his face. Slowly move the toy from side to side, keeping pace with his ability to track the object with his eyes.

• Try slowly lifting the object up and down so he can watch it moving from near to far. Touch the toy to his torso, or use it to stroke his face and arms. Of course, you shouldn't leave the baby unattended with small objects.

SKILL SPOTLIGHT

Watching a brightly colored *object move from side to side and up and down helps strengthen your baby's eye muscles so that he can track objects and focus at different distances, a skill that requires "visual convergence," or having the two eyes working together. Feeling the pom-poms gently touch his torso, face, and limbs lets him explore textures.*

✔	**Tactile Stimulation**
✔	**Visual Development**
✔	**Visual Tracking**

A BRIGHT YELLOW POM-POM is intriguing to a baby, especially when it brushes his skin.

21

INFANT MASSAGE

TOUCHING TO RELAX

SKILLSPOTLIGHT

Touch is deeply reassuring *for infants, especially if it's done calmly and gently. A mild massage stimulates your baby's circulation, sense of touch, and awareness of her body. Looking at and talking to your baby helps to strengthen your all-important emotional bond.*

Body Awareness	✔
Emotional Development	✔
Social Development	✔
Tactile Stimulation	✔

CULTURES AROUND THE WORLD have practiced various forms of infant massage for thousands of years. Classes and books are available on this topic, but you can do very simple forms of massage at home with your baby, too. Find a warm room or a sunny spot on the bed or carpet, and a time when you're relaxed and your baby is receptive. Take off all her clothes and rub oil between your hands to prevent friction and make the massage pleasing. Use a vegetable-based oil, such as grapeseed or safflower oil; avoid baby oil and other petroleum-based products.

• Using a milking motion, gently squeeze down each arm and leg. Then move your hands from the center of her torso out to the sides. Or softly brush your fingertips over her skin. Speak or sing to her at the same time.

• Place your fingers on her temples and make very small, gentle circles. Then place your fingertips in the middle of her forehead and draw them slowly along her eyebrows. Try gently moving your thumbs along the bridge of her nose, down around her nostrils, and to the corners of her mouth.

SHE LOVES TO FEEL YOUR TOUCH, see your eyes, and hear your voice.

RESEARCH REPORT

"Touch," writes Theresa Caplain in the classic The First Twelve Months of Life, *"is almost a language for infants."* Indeed, numerous studies have shown that touching your baby – holding her, kissing her, and stroking her – helps deepen bonding. It can also help her physiologically. Research shows that babies who are touched have increased immune functions, improved muscle development, and greater production of growth hormones.

R E S E A R C H REPORT

Parents' faces and sounds *don't just entertain the baby; they can actually make him feel more secure. A study at the University of Delaware found that the infants of mothers who had more animated facial expressions were more securely attached to their mothers than those who did not. And numerous studies of depressed or withdrawn mothers have found that their infants also tend to be less attached and expressive.*

LOOKING TIME is bonding time when it's gentle and responsive.

FACIAL EXPRESSIONS

FROM BIRTH
0
AND UP

LOOKING, LEARNING, LOVING

NOT ALL THE ACTIVITIES you do with your baby have to be vigorous — or even active. Quiet time is equally important. Babies, especially newborns, are easily overstimulated. And intimacy between parent and child depends as much on touch and eye contact as it does on giggles, tickles, and toys. In other words, time spent simply gazing into your baby's eyes is time well spent, as it allows the two of you a chance to relax and bond.

• Choose a time when your infant is alert and receptive. Cradle him in your arms, prop him up on your knees, or lay him down on the changing table or a soft blanket on the floor.

• When he's looking at you, gaze into his eyes. Speak or sing his name softly. Introduce him to some facial expressions: a smile, an opened mouth, raised eyebrows, a stuck-out tongue. Then go back to simply looking at him and saying his name softly.

• Your baby may surprise you by imitating your expressions; even the littlest babies will sometimes mirror the face of a caregiver. But if he grows restless or turns away repeatedly, stop the activity. Babies need to withdraw from intense interactions to process all they've experienced.

IF YOUR BABY ENJOYS THIS ACTIVITY, also try Who Is That?, page 30. ▶

SKILLSPOTLIGHT

You may have noticed *that your baby began scanning your face — or moving his eyes from your hairline to your chin — almost as soon as he was born. That's evidence that faces are very, very important to young babies. Having time in which he can simply look at your face and its expressions lets him begin to make important attachments and learn social cues for affection.*

✔	**Emotional Development**
✔	**Listening**
✔	**Social Development**
✔	**Visual Development**

LULLABIES

IT'S HARD TO SAY why simple melodies soothe infants, but generation upon generation of parents have sung songs to their little ones, and generation upon generation of little ones have thus been lulled. Lots of lullabies just seem to beg babies to fall asleep, but any quiet song, sung lovingly, can induce sleep, or at least settle an overstimulated baby.

CRADLE SONG

 to the *tune* of **Brahms' Lullaby**

**Lullaby, and good night –
go to sleep little baby.
Close your eyes now
sweetly rest.
May your slumbers be blessed.
Close your eyes now
sweetly rest.
May your slumbers be blessed.**

WHETHER IT COMES from an older sibling or a parent, a tender song is a time-honored way of calming infants.

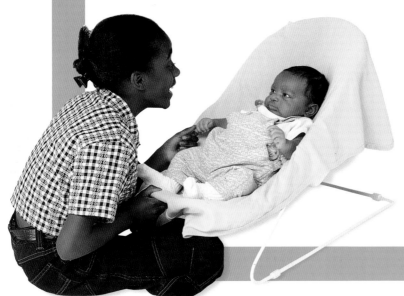

HUSH, LITTLE BABY

Hush, little baby, don't say a word,
Papa's gonna buy you a mockingbird.

And if that mockingbird won't sing,
Papa's gonna buy you a diamond ring.

If that diamond ring turns brass,
Papa's gonna buy you a looking glass.

If that looking glass gets broke,
Papa's gonna buy you a billy goat.

If that billy goat don't pull,
Papa's gonna buy you a cart and bull.

If that cart and bull turn over,
Papa's gonna buy you a dog named
Rover.

If that dog named Rover don't bark,
Papa's gonna buy you a horse and cart.

If that horse and cart fall down,
you'll still be the sweetest little
baby in town.

ALL THE PRETTY HORSES

Hush a bye, don't you cry,
go to sleep little baby.

When you wake, you shall have
all the pretty little horses.

Blacks and bays, dapples and grays,
all the pretty little horses.

Hush a bye, don't you cry,
go to sleep little baby.

SINGING A SONG to put
your baby to sleep is soothing
to both you and your infant.

27

FROM BIRTH 0 AND UP

HANKIE WAVE

A TRACKING GAME

SKILLSPOTLIGHT

Watching the cloth wave *back and forth at this age will boost your baby's ability to visually track and focus on objects. But by three months, she won't be able to resist reaching out and trying to grab the cloth. And by six months, she'll be gumming the cloth as soon as she gets it into her tiny grasp.*

Listening	✔
Visual Stimulation	✔

ONE OF THE BEST-KEPT SECRETS about playing with young babies is that you don't always need fancy toys with electronic bells and whistles. In fact, sometimes just a cloth, handkerchief, or colorful scarf will do. Place your baby on her back on the floor or changing table. Hold a scarf, handkerchief, or lightweight cloth about twelve inches over her head. Bring it close to her, then lift it farther away, and bring it down again. Sing to her or call her name as you wave the cloth.

A SCARF OR CLOTH creates a tickling breeze and an intriguing visual object for your little one to follow. Be sure to put it away when playtime is over.

CRYING AND COLIC

YOUR BABY'S CRY will become as familiar to you as the shapes of his toes. That won't make dealing with it any easier. Some days you'll feel nothing but sympathy; other days your patience will be pushed to its limits.

Babies cry in response to unpleasant experiences, including hunger, loneliness, fatigue, pain, or being chilled or overheated. Some researchers also believe that at three to six weeks, some babies start crying in the early evening simply to let off steam after a long day.

A "colicky" baby cries more persistently and more often than others. Researchers don't know the cause of colic. Colicky babies may have immature digestive systems, or they may just have a harder time dealing with the world's stimuli. Whatever the cause, even the most loving parents can feel inadequate, anxious, or even angry when faced with the nonstop, shrill cries of a colicky baby.

Some people may tell you to let your baby "cry it out." Most pediatricians these days would disagree.

Comforting your baby — or at least trying to comfort him — shows him that he can count on you to respond and that distress eventually ends.

What you can do for your baby: If burping, changing, or feeding your baby doesn't help, try motion (such as walking with the baby in a stroller or front pack, or rocking, dancing, or swinging). Fresh air can quiet a crying baby. And young babies often appreciate being swaddled.

What you can do for yourself: Try to catch up on missed sleep. Fatigue makes parents more vulnerable to depression and short tempers, which can make it hard to respond wholeheartedly to your baby's cries. Ask someone else to watch the baby while you take a shower or go out for a walk. Don't feel you're abandoning your baby. Think of it as replenishing your diminished resources. ■

29

"Who's that little baby?"

WHO IS THAT?

SELF-REFLECTIONS

NEWBORNS ARE MORE ATTUNED to real human faces than to any other visual object, including rattles, geometric shapes, or even drawings of human faces. In her earliest weeks, a baby stares at faces even though she doesn't know that they, like her, are human. That means she'll be fascinated by her own tiny reflection in a handheld mirror – even though she'll have no idea who it is. Hold a mirror up so your baby can see her reflection. Point at the baby in the mirror, and say her name. As she grows older her reflection will prompt that first sign of sociability – the infant's impish grin.

A MIRROR PROVIDES a fun-filled play experience for the whole family.

SKILL SPOTLIGHT

A baby won't recognize herself *in the mirror until she's around fifteen months old. But even in her earliest months, gazing at herself in the mirror helps her learn to visually focus and track as well as to explore the social nature of faces. Eventually, it will help her identify herself as both a baby and a unique being.*

✔ **Emotional Development**

✔ **Social Development**

✔ **Visual Development**

IF YOUR BABY ENJOYS THIS ACTIVITY, also try Facial Expressions, page 24.

FROM BIRTH AND UP
0

AIRPLANE BABY

SOARING TO NEW HEIGHTS

SKILLSPOTLIGHT

Parents around the world *have spent many long hours comforting colicky babies by swinging them gently back and forth in an "airplane" hold. The steady pressure along the baby's tummy provides soothing warmth and tactile input. And with every passing week she'll practice lifting her head, neck, and shoulders so that she can look around and widen her baby's-eye view.*

Tactile Stimulation	✔
Trust	✔
Upper-Body Strength	✔

YOU MAY ALREADY have discovered that a classic "airplane" or "football" hold calms your baby when she's gassy, overwhelmed, or just tired. Combining a swinging or swaying motion and a rhythmic song with that firm hold around her belly can be even more calming. Just support your baby, tummy down, by holding her under her chest and belly with one or both of your arms. (But always be sure to support a newborn's head.) Then swing her gently to and fro while singing a song.

WITH A LITTLE BIT OF WIND in her little bit of hair and with Mommy's arm supporting her, she's soaring like a glider.

TICKLE-ME TEXTURES

TELLING TACTILE TALES

NEWBORNS DON'T ALWAYS LIKE to be undressed because the air feels cold on their skin. Older babies often fuss during diaper changes because they don't want to be restrained. You can turn changing time into play and learning time by providing your baby with interesting tactile experiences.

• Gather several objects with different textures. Try swatches of velvet and corduroy, feathers, or a clean sponge dampened with warm water.

• Gently rub an object across your baby's skin and watch for her response. Try a different object. Look for clues that indicate her preferences.

• This is an activity that can entertain your baby for many months. Sometime after her ninth month, she may find the texture toys and hold them out for you to tickle her with!

SKILLSPOTLIGHT

Your baby's skin *is about as alive to touch now as it ever will be because touch is one of the baby's primary ways of exploring the world. This activity introduces her to a wide range of the world's textures. It also gives you a chance to practice recognizing and responding to her body language. Such attuned responses help build her sense of security as she witnesses her needs being taken care of.*

✔	**Body Awareness**
✔	**Social Development**
✔	**Tactile Stimulation**

THE FEATHERY TEXTURE makes her squirm with pleasure.

IF YOUR BABY ENJOYS THIS ACTIVITY, also try Infant Massage, page 22.

33

CRADLE SONGS

YOUR **BABY** won't actually giggle at a tickle until he's about three months old. Tactile games will intrigue him, however, and will boost his budding awareness of his own body. And incorporating silly songs or chants will appeal to his innate fascination with the human voice.

YOUR TOUCH and the sound of your voice are all he needs to have fun.

DID YOU EVER SEE A LASSIE

**Did you ever see a lassie,
a lassie, a lassie,
did you ever see a lassie
go this way and that?**
*walk your fingers slowly back and forth
across baby's body*

**Go this way and that way,
go this way and that way,
did you ever see a lassie
go this way and that?**
*walk your fingers slowly back and forth
across baby's body*

YANKEE DOODLE

Yankee Doodle went to town
a-riding on a pony;
stuck a feather in his cap
and called it macaroni.

Yankee Doodle keep it up,
Yankee Doodle dandy;
mind the music and the step
and with the girls be handy.

TWINKLE, TWINKLE LITTLE STAR

Twinkle, twinkle little star,
hold hands up, opening and closing fists
how I wonder what you are!

Up above the world so high,
point upward
like a diamond in the sky.
*create a diamond with thumbs
and forefingers*

Twinkle, twinkle little star,
open and close fists
how I wonder what you are!

LITTLE PETER RABBIT

 to the *tune* of "John Brown's Body"

Little Peter Rabbit had a fly
upon his nose.
touch baby's nose

Little Peter Rabbit had a fly
upon his nose.
touch baby's nose

Little Peter Rabbit had a fly
upon his nose.
touch baby's nose

And he flipped it,
and he flopped it
*"shoo" fly near
baby's face*

till it flew away.
make flying motion

HEARING A SIMPLE SONG
when in Daddy's arms is
always a delight.

GETTING ORGANIZED

WHEN YOUR BABY is born, your home is filled with the presence of a precious new being. It also gets filled with a whole lot of baby "stuff." It's not just the crib, stroller, and changing table you bought before the baby's due date. Before you know it, your home will also be bursting with everything from tiny clothes and diapers to bottles and toys.

Having a perfectly tidy house isn't the top priority of most new parents. But adapting your expectations and household organizing systems should be. Remember that you can't get as much done as you did in pre-baby days. Be flexible. Make lists, but don't berate yourself for not completing every task.

At your fingertips: Diapers, diaper wipes, rash ointment, and clothing should be kept within arm's reach of the changing table so you don't leave the baby unattended. And baby washcloths, soaps, and towels should be close by at bath time.

Put like with like: You can use baskets or plastic boxes to keep toys sorted. Keeping clothes organized by size and season — all of the things that fit now in the top drawer, and all of the things that are too big but might fit by summer in another — also helps. Having a system makes it easier for you — and any other caretakers — to find the right clothes quickly.

For a rainy, or later, day: You don't have to put out every toy, book, and article of clothing you receive. Toys meant for an eighteen-month-old can be stored; you'll be glad to have some fresh toys when the time comes. Older-baby clothing can be sorted and tucked away in a closet.

Tidy up: You can't expect to have all the household chores done all the time. But you can decide to do one job once a day. Whether you do it in the evening or during the baby's afternoon nap, having the house somewhat neat can be a balm for a parent's soul. ■

RIPPLING RIBBONS

VISIONS OF LOVELINESS

LONG BEFORE YOUR BABY is eagerly tearing paper off packages, ribbons will capture her curiosity and attention. Using masking tape, attach six-inch lengths of brightly colored ribbon to a piece of cardboard, or tie them securely to a wooden spoon. Lay your baby on the floor or changing table, or in an infant car seat. Then gently wave the ribbons around her face and hands. When she starts kicking her feet and jerking her arms, you'll know she's having fun with the colors, textures, and movement.

SKILLSPOTLIGHT

At this age, *watching the ribbons dance up and down and from side to side helps your baby develop her visual tracking skills. When she is older and starts swiping at objects, this activity lets her practice her eye-hand coordination and grasping skills, and lets her see the relationship between cause (I hit the ribbon) and effect (The ribbon swings and bounces).*

✔ **Eye-Hand Coordination**

✔ **Tactile Stimulation**

✔ **Visual Development**

SHE'S NOT QUITE OLD ENOUGH to reach out and grasp yet, but she still loves the movement.

SOUND SPOTS

WHERE'S MOMMY'S VOICE?

SKILLSPOTLIGHT

Listening and looking *for your voice helps your baby develop both his visual tracking and auditory location skills. Equally important is your introduction of the idea that his family provides smiles, laughter, and praise. By the time he's six months old, he, too, will be smiling and laughing, and by the time he's one year old, he'll be trying to get you to turn your head toward him when he makes funny sounds.*

BABIES ARE BORN with an innate fascination with human voices, but they're not born with an immediate ability to locate the source of a sound in a room. To help your baby fine-tune his senses, try this: Place him in a car seat or infant chair in the middle of a room. Walk back and forth in front of him as you sing songs, make funny noises, or talk to him. Then try walking to the opposite side of the room and back again, letting him follow the sound of your voice. Although he won't turn his head at the sound of your voice, he'll hear the difference in sound as you move back and forth.

Listening	✔
Social Development	✔
Visual Development	✔

IF YOUR BABY ENJOYS THIS ACTIVITY, also try Noisemakers, page 44.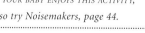

Most parents get a kick *out of claiming that their infant's personality – be it calm, restless, sweet, or belligerent – was foretold by his activity in the womb. But do such links between prenatal behavior and post-natal personality have any merit? In fact, researchers at Johns Hopkins University have found that several factors, including heart rate and movement in the womb, really can help predict what an infant's temperament will be during his first few months. According to the study, more active fetuses generally turn into more lively and unpredictable infants.*

FINDING MOMMY'S VOICE will eventually evolve into fun games of peekaboo and hide-and-go-seek.

FROM BIRTH
0
AND UP

EYES ON TRACK

SPOT THE TOY

SKILL SPOTLIGHT

What's that sound? *What's that movement? As your baby moves her head from side to side, she learns to locate the source of noises and keep track of an object's whereabouts. At around three months, she'll swipe at the toy, and at about four months she'll grab at it.*

| Listening | ✔ |
| Visual Tracking | ✔ |

▶ *IF YOUR BABY ENJOYS THIS ACTIVITY, also try Rippling Ribbons, page 37.*

EVEN AS NEWBORNS, babies display interest in sights and sounds. Try moving a brightly colored squeaking toy back and forth slowly in front of your baby's eyes. When she's focused on the toy, move it to the left and to the right. Don't go too fast or far afield, though. If she loses sight of the toy, she'll figure it simply doesn't exist, and she'll lose interest in the game altogether.

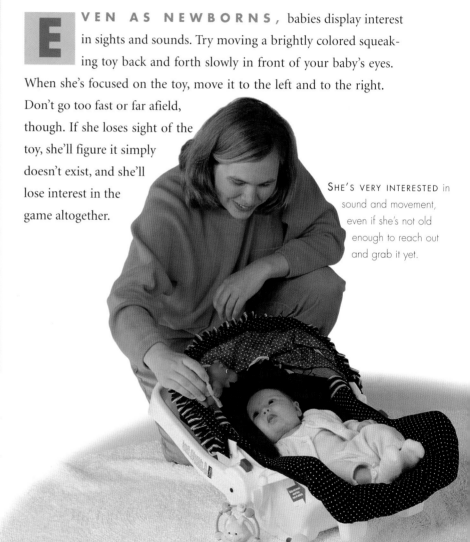

SHE'S VERY INTERESTED in sound and movement, even if she's not old enough to reach out and grab it yet.

ROCK THE BABY

FROM BIRTH
0
AND UP

BALANCE ON A BOLSTER

WHEN WE THINK OF ROCKING, we usually think of a baby on her back in a cradle or in our arms in a rocking chair. But one very soothing motion for an infant is to be gently rocked from side to side on her tummy. Roll up a towel or two together. Lay your baby on her stomach over the roll so that it supports her head, chest, stomach, and thighs. Turn her head to one side. Then very gently rock her from side to side while singing a song such as "Rock the Baby" (see the lyrics at right). The rocking motion helps her develop a sense of balance, while lying on her tummy gives her a chance to try to lift her head from a belly-down position.

THE PRESSURE on her tummy can be soothing; the rocking motion helps her gain an elementary sense of balance.

Rock the Baby

to the *tune* of **"London Bridge Is Falling Down"**

**Rock the baby
side to side,
side to side,
side to side.
Rock the baby
side to side,
just like this.**

✔ **Balance**

✔ **Spatial Awareness**

✔ **Upper-Body Strength**

IF YOUR BABY ENJOYS THIS ACTIVITY, also try Beach-Ball Balance, page 42.

BEACH-BALL BALANCE

A ROCK AND ROLL GAME

SKILLSPOTLIGHT

Rolling back and forth *and from side to side stimulates baby's sense of balance. After the first month, most babies will also try to lift up their heads to see what's going on around them. That helps build upper-body strength. And the gentle pressure on the tummy can help babies with gas or colic.*

Balance	✔
Trust	✔
Upper-Body Strength	✔

YOUNG BABIES often don't like to lie on their tummies for very long. But most find it pretty interesting to lie on something big, soft, and round for a little while. Try placing your baby tummy-down on a slightly deflated beach ball. (But always be sure to support a newborn's head.) Turn her head to one side. Then, while securely holding her, rock her slowly forward and back or side to side on the ball. Sing or talk to her while you play; that will help keep her focused while the gentle rhythm and pressure soothe her tummy. Stop when she gets tired. When she's older and nearly able to sit up on her own, you can support her seated on top of the beach ball, and very gently bounce her up and down.

BRIGHT COLORS, a squishy surface, and a delightful rolling sensation make a winning combination.

IF YOUR BABY ENJOYS THIS ACTIVITY, also try Rock the Baby, page 41.

"Rock and roll, baby!"

NOISEMAKERS

SOUND SENSATIONS

SKILLSPOTLIGHT

Hearing the various sounds *from the dangling objects will sharpen your baby's auditory awareness and his visual discrimination skills. Seeing the objects will help him focus. And in a few months, when your baby is able to swipe at objects, this activity can encourage him to develop his gross motor skills.*

Eye-Hand Coordination	✓
Listening	✓
Visual Development	✓

WHETHER THE SOUND is familiar, like that of a musical mobile, or unfamiliar, like a new voice, noises intrigue even the very youngest babies. Create a primitive symphony of sound by stringing a number of noise-making objects — jar lids, lightweight rattles, or plastic and wooden spoons — on a rope or ribbon. Dangle and shake the noisemaker about twelve inches in front of your baby. Or string it across the crib and let him gaze up at it as you shake the rope or jiggle the objects for him, just don't leave him alone with this kind of toy.

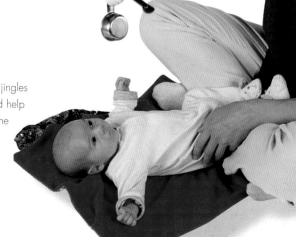

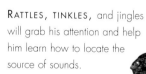

RATTLES, TINKLES, and jingles will grab his attention and help him learn how to locate the source of sounds.

LITTLE BIRD WATCHERS

FROM BIRTH
0
AND UP

BABY'S FIRST NATURE CLASS

A **FLUTTER OF WINGS,** a flash of color, a sharp whistle or trill — such sights and sounds will fascinate almost any baby. The challenge, of course, is getting her close enough to actually see the birds. Try placing a bird feeder filled with seed just outside a window. As the birds begin to flock, hold your baby up so she can see them, or place her infant seat where she can watch them come and go. Soon she'll be crowing delightedly when she sees her feathered friends.

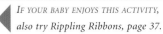

SHE LOVES TO WATCH these funny flying creatures flit about.

SKILLSPOTLIGHT

A newborn will have trouble *seeing the birds clearly, but she may detect a blur of color or motion. Over the next few months, watching birds will help her develop her visual tracking and focusing abilities. Her curiosity about the birds is a great example of her blossoming fascination with the world around her. A year from now — believe it or not — she'll be begging to help you fill the feeder!*

 Listening

 Visual Development

◄ IF YOUR BABY ENJOYS THIS ACTIVITY, *also try Rippling Ribbons, page 37.*

BABYCYCLE

A BODY-AWARENESS ACTIVITY

SKILL SPOTLIGHT

By moving his legs *for him, you let your baby feel his little legs and feet moving in a new way — each side of the body working in reciprocal movement. You also mimic an action he'll be using later on as he learns to crawl.*

Body Awareness	✔
Gross Motor Skills	✔

◀ *IF YOUR BABY ENJOYS THIS ACTIVITY, also try Infant Massage, page 22.*

WHEN HE'S FIRST BORN, your baby has no idea that his body is actually separate from yours. But his expanding physical abilities will give rise to an increased interest in his own body parts that will last him well into toddlerhood. They also let him enjoy more physical, interactive games. In this simple exercise game, you very gently and very slowly move his legs in a bicycling motion, all the while talking and smiling at him to encourage him to wiggle his legs without your help. Before you know it he'll be grabbing his own little feet — and eventually pedaling all by himself!

IT FEELS GOOD to stretch and kick —especially when Mommy's guiding the movement.

"Look at those legs go!"

STRETCHING OUT

GENTLE GYM

I'm a Tiny Baby

 to the *tune* of "Itsy-Bitsy Spider"

I'm a tiny baby
I'm soft and round and small.
But when I'm busy stretching
I feel so big and tall.
My arms are getting long, and my legs are getting strong.
And the next thing you know,
I'll be learning how to crawl.

| Body Awareness | ✔ |
| Tactile Stimulation | ✔ |

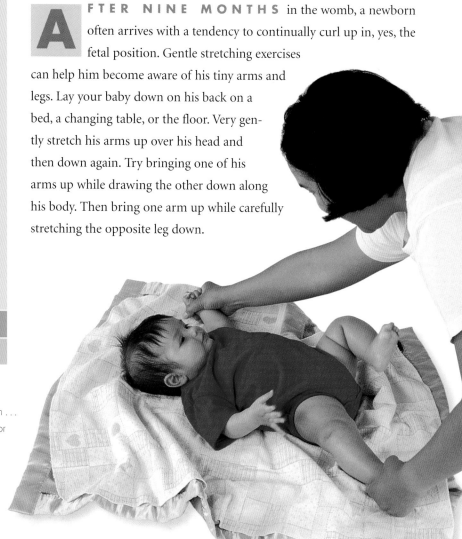

AFTER NINE MONTHS in the womb, a newborn often arrives with a tendency to continually curl up in, yes, the fetal position. Gentle stretching exercises can help him become aware of his tiny arms and legs. Lay your baby down on his back on a bed, a changing table, or the floor. Very gently stretch his arms up over his head and then down again. Try bringing one of his arms up while drawing the other down along his body. Then bring one arm up while carefully stretching the opposite leg down.

ONE ARM UP, one leg down . . . gentle stretching is relaxing for babies and parents alike.

48

SWAT THE TOY

CATCH AS CATCH CAN

YOUR BABY may be able to see (at close range) as well as you can, but her ability to grasp objects is still not a match for yours. To help her, attach a small plush toy or teething ring to a brightly colored ribbon or plastic links. Dangle the toy in front of her and make it sway from side to side, encouraging her to reach across her body. Praise her efforts as she reaches out and swipes at— or even grabs— the toy. But never leave a baby alone with a long ribbon, as it poses a safety hazard.

WHEN YOUR BABY is grasping a pink plush puppy, she is exercising her ability to reach out and make contact with her world.

SKILL SPOTLIGHT

By three months, *most babies are using their heads and eyes together to track moving objects. That is, if an object moves to the left, the baby rotates her head to the left to follow the object, rather than just moving her eyes, as a newborn does. But she still needs to practice her grasping skills. Reaching for a moving object helps her fine-tune the coordination of both sides of her body.*

✔	**Eye-Hand Coordination**
✔	**Fine Motor Skills**
✔	**Visual Development**

IF YOUR BABY ENJOYS THIS ACTIVITY, also try Big Bouncing Ball, page 80.

49

3 MONTHS
3
AND UP

TARGET PRACTICE

A KICKING GAME

SKILLSPOTLIGHT

For babies, *eye-foot coordination is important. Eventually, using the feet in conjunction with the eyes will help him cruise the furniture and learn to walk.*

HE'S ALREADY DISCOVERED the joy of kicking his little legs. Give your baby's kicking a purpose by holding a target for him to try to hit. When he's on his back — on the changing table, a bed, or the floor — hold up a pillow, a plush toy, your hands, or a pie tin within easy reach of his little feet. If he doesn't understand the game, guide his feet to the target and praise him when he makes contact. Once he figures out what to do, he'll want to practice this one over and over.

Body Awareness	✔
Eye-Foot Coordination	✔
Listening	✔

HE SEES HIS FOOT make contact, he hears the resulting noise, and he feels the sole of his foot on the plate.

50

PEEKABOO GAMES

VARIATIONS ON A THEME

FIRST MOMMY'S THERE, then Mommy's gone, and then she's back again. Peekaboo is a perennial favorite with babies. Sometime around six or seven months, babies start to understand that objects continue to exist even when they are not present. Peekaboo is a great way to explore this concept with your little one. You can hold a blanket or diaper in front of your face while you say "Where's Mommy? Where's Mommy?" and then peek out from behind. Or put a light towel over your baby's face instead, then whisk it off, calling, "Peekaboo!" when her face emerges.

SKILLSPOTLIGHT

A newborn baby thinks *that when an object disappears, it no longer exists. When you appear and disappear behind the diaper, she begins to learn that even if you're momentarily hidden, you're still there. Grasping this concept – i.e., holding mental images – is a precursor to language development. When she gets old enough to put a blanket over her own face (albeit haphazardly), you'll see her kick and squirm with joy, as she's now in control of the disappearing act.*

 Object Permanence

 Social Development

"PEEKABOO!" It's a relief and a revelation for her to realize you never really left at all.

51

BABBLING WITH BABY

THE LITTLEST LANGUAGE LESSONS

SKILLSPOTLIGHT

Responding to your baby's *babbling supports his early efforts to communicate using sounds other than crying. Reinforcement of his vocalizations will show him that people value what he has to say, which will make it more rewarding for him to master language in the long run.*

Language Development	✔
Listening	✔
Social Development	✔

IF YOUR BABY ENJOYS THIS ACTIVITY, also try Fingerpuppet Fun, page 97. ▶

A THREE- TO SIX-MONTH-OLD BABY is often a delightfully social little being full of funny coos, gurgles, shouts, grunts, and irresistible smiles. Although he can't say real words yet (that won't come until he's nearing his first birthday), he utters those adorable sounds as a way of exploring the sounds he hears every day. He also learns from the responses you give to these vocalizations. Encourage his early efforts by holding a baby-babble conversation with him.

• When he says "aaah," listen, nod, and say "aaah" in return. When he says "goo!" you say "goo!" too.

• Once you're both warmed up, try changing his words slightly, by stretching them out ("bah!" becomes "baaaaaaah") or even adding to them ("ooh" becomes "oooh-wah!").

• Encouraging your baby to mimic you will inspire him to try ever more complex language patterns, which eventually will result in his attempting words and then phrases.

Note: This kind of baby talk is constructive only until a child begins talking. At that point, it's better to repeat words correctly than repeat his incorrect pronunciations, no matter how cute they are.

RESEARCH REPORT

For the first six months, *babies will babble whether you talk to them or not. But they'll learn how to talk more easily if you make a concerted effort to show them how language works. Indeed, all babies – no matter what language is spoken in their home – sound alike until they're about six months old. After that, they start repeating the sounds they hear most often around them.*

HE'LL SQUEAL AND SQUIRM when he realizes you're following his lead in this elementary conversation.

SLEEPING THROUGH THE NIGHT

BY THE TIME she's three or four months old, your baby will probably have developed some sort of sleep pattern. It may be a dream-come-true sleep pattern, or it may feel like your biggest life challenge – waking every hour on the hour at night, never napping for more than half an hour during the day, suddenly getting daytime (wake time) and nighttime (sleep time) reversed, or something in between.

Getting a baby to sleep on a "normal" schedule is actually a matter of common sense and logistics, with a little bravery and patience thrown in.

Develop a daytime routine: plan fairly regular times for outings, baths, play periods, and meals. External regularity will help her set her inner clock.

Develop a nighttime routine: a warm bath, cozy pajamas, a lullaby, and some books are classic ways of getting your baby to unwind. It's never too early to convince a baby that nighttime feedings are all business and kind of boring. Keep the lights low, don't talk to her very much, don't let her play with toys or watch television, and gently put her in her crib on her back as soon as she's done.

Once your baby is about six months old, she shouldn't really need to eat during the night. Some parents choose to use a modified "cry it out" program, letting her cry for a few minutes, then going in to reassure her, then letting her cry some more; some may continue to feed, cuddle, walk, or sing to their babies in hopes that eventually the child will sleep longer and longer on her own. Eventually, most babies will learn to put themselves to sleep, which is an important skill to have.

What's the best approach? It's a little bit different for every family. The magic formula is the method that you and your baby feel most comfortable with – and that's a personal decision. ◼

TUMMY BOLSTER

BUILDING UPPER-BODY STRENGTH

LEARNING HOW TO SIT requires far more than just keeping one's head up; it also calls on the muscles of the shoulders, torso, and upper and lower back. You can help your baby develop those muscles by bolstering him with a rolled-up towel, the ends secured with soft fabric hair bands. Slip the towel roll under his arms and chest while he lies on his tummy on the floor or carpet. The bolster helps him to raise his neck and shoulders up for longer periods and encourages him to use his arms for support. It also offers him an enticing view of the world around him.

SKILLSPOTLIGHT

Using a bolster *like this one helps your baby practice putting weight on his forearms, which helps him strengthen his arm and back muscles in preparation for sitting up and eventually crawling. And giving him a new position from which to view the world will stimulate his vision and inspire him to reach, roll, or even creep forward.*

✔	**Emotional Development**
✔	**Social Development**
✔	**Upper-Body Strength**

HE'LL GET a new perspective on his world perched up on his chest this way.

IF YOUR BABY ENJOYS THIS ACTIVITY, also try Tummy Talk, page 60.

55

FRIENDLY FACES

A BOOK OF MUG SHOTS

SKILLSPOTLIGHT

The combination *of your baby's visual abilities and desire for human interaction makes her highly sensitive to cues provided by facial expressions. A book full of different faces gives her many to contemplate. She may simply stare at them – glancing from their eyes to their mouths and back again. Or she may try to point or talk to the pictures.*

MAKING YOUR OWN

You can create a face book by gluing photos (either from magazines or from your own collection) on pieces of heavy cardboard. Preserve them with clear plastic contact paper or sheet protectors. Or simply place photos in a photo album.

BY THE AGE OF THREE MONTHS, your baby is so attuned to facial expressions that she responds to smiles or laughter. She can also tell the difference between her loved ones' faces and unfamiliar faces. That's why you get that special grin when your baby peers at you over someone else's shoulder and your friends just get a solemn gaze. It's also why her whole body wriggles when you peek at her over her crib rail in the morning; she recognizes your face, and she already loves it dearly.

Giving your baby a book with lots of faces – either one you buy or one you make – introduces your baby to a wide range of faces and the many emotions they express. You may even find that she develops favorites – perhaps the little boy gleefully holding a puppy, or the picture of Daddy looking sheepish in his fishing hat.

Social Development	✔
Visual Discrimination	✔

POINTING OUT THE PEOPLE in the pictures helps your baby begin to connect names with familiar faces.

MIRROR PLAY

WHO'S THAT BABY?

SKILLSPOTLIGHT

Watching her own face *and interacting with her image in the mirror increases your baby's budding awareness of herself as a separate person. And if she lies on her stomach, it will help her strengthen the muscles needed for sitting and crawling.*

| Upper-Body Strength | ✔ |
| Visual Stimulation | ✔ |

◄ *IF YOUR BABY ENJOYS THIS ACTIVITY, also try Facial Expressions, page 24.*

A **THREE- OR FOUR-MONTH-OLD BABY** is just getting to the point where she can amuse herself for several minutes on end — an exciting breakthrough for baby and parents alike. You may hear her gurgling to her toes early in the morning, for instance; see her fiddling with her hands in front of her face; or catch her looking intently around a room. At around four months old, a baby can not only see but also track, which means that she can actually watch objects or people as they move around her. Now that your baby can lift her head while she's on her tummy, a mirror in her crib can provide a lot of fun. She doesn't yet understand that she's looking at herself in the mirror, and she won't until she's fifteen to eighteen months old. Still, she'll brighten and smile when she sees her own face — she's happy to be greeted by such an intriguing person!

YOUR BABY will be enchanted by her new playmate, even if she doesn't recognize it is her own image. Be sure to remove the mirror from the crib when she's done.

TUMMY TALK

STRENGTHENING THE NECK AND BACK

SKILLSPOTLIGHT

Every moment your baby spends on his tummy helps build up his strength. Your reassuring presence and pride in his accomplishments (however small) also help him learn that it's really OK to be on his stomach. When you roll him back over when he gets too uncomfortable (as indeed you should), he learns yet again that someone is paying attention to his cues and responding appropriately.

Emotional Development	✔
Social Development	✔
Upper-Body Strength	✔

AT THREE MONTHS, some babies may still cry in protest when placed on their tummies. But spending time in that position is crucial, as it helps them to strengthen the neck, shoulder, and back muscles in preparation for sitting and crawling.

• You shouldn't make your baby stay in a position he is not comfortable with, but you can persuade him to like it more by lying in front of him, placing a favorite toy in view, making eye contact, and socializing with him a bit.

• Encourage him if he starts improvising on the position. He may start "swimming" excitedly with his arms and legs, for instance. Or he may stiffen them in an "airplane" position and rock back and forth.

• Don't worry if he can only tolerate being on his belly for a minute or two. Follow his lead and quit when he's had enough. You can try again later. Plenty of babies are challenged by tummy time – and all of them learn to sit, crawl, and walk.

IF MOMMY'S DOING IT, then he may decide it's OK for him to try it awhile, too.

60

"Here's looking at you, kid."

RESEARCHREPORT

You may be aware *of the concern of some doctors that sleeping on the back (currently advised for preventing "crib death" or Sudden Infant Death Syndrome) may slow babies' gross motor skill development because their neck and back muscles don't get as much exercise. In fact, recent research shows that while some back sleepers roll over and crawl later than tummy sleepers, both types learn to walk at about the same age.*

GETTING OTHERS INVOLVED

IT'S A FACT that in most families, Mommy takes on the lion's share of the care for young babies. Unfortunately, the more Mommy does it, the more she — and everyone else — starts feeling that she's the only one who knows how to do it right. Here are a few ways to help others get involved with your baby's care and play.

The other parent: If Mom stays at home and Dad goes to work, she changes ten times as many diapers as he does, prepares three times as many meals, and spends about eight times as long playing with the baby. If they're both working, statistics show, she's still spending more time with the baby. That can make her feel like she's the expert and him feel that he's all thumbs.

How do you let go? Tell your significant other what he needs to know for safety's sake (for example, the baby can now roll off the bed), and then walk away and let him figure it out. If he secures a diaper too loosely or puts the baby in a position she doesn't like, he'll soon discover his mistake.

Grandparents: They may have different or outdated ideas about child rearing, or have forgotten how to take care of a baby. But a grandparent's love is special and something your child shouldn't miss. Explaining what works and is safe for your baby will make everyone feel more comfortable. Let them know what your baby enjoys, and then let them indulge their love.

Baby-sitters: Regular baby-sitters will have a good idea of what toys your baby enjoys, what comforts her, and what trouble she's attracted to. Occasional baby-sitters need to have that information spelled out. Show all baby-sitters where extra bottles and clothing and the first-aid kit are kept. Leave emergency telephone numbers. Then leave! It's important for parents and babies alike to know that little ones are safe in the care of other adults. ■

PINWHEEL MAGIC

BLOWING IN THE WIND

BY FOUR MONTHS, your baby's vision has developed significantly, he can control his head, and he's starting to reach out to touch things. This means he's ready – and eager – to take in the wonders of the wide world. Try showing him the blur of beautiful colors that results when you blow on a pinwheel. He himself won't be able to blow on it until he's more than a year old, but he may enjoy watching you wave it in the air. (Most babies this age will try to grab at pinwheels. Don't let them, however, as the sharp edges could hurt them and small pieces could be swallowed.) You can also place the pinwheel outside in a planter box and seat your baby near it so that he can watch the colors go round.

SKILL SPOTLIGHT

A tantalizing pinwheel *will mesmerize most babies. A younger baby – around three months – will be fascinated by the blur of movement and may swipe vaguely at the pinwheel with closed fists. By six months, though, he'll be able to see and reach for the pinwheel. You can also sing a spinning pinwheel song to add to the fun.*

✔	**Social Development**
✔	**Visual Development**

GRANDPA'S colorful pinwheel will capture the baby's attention and possibly prompt a gleeful reaction.

63

TICK-TOCK

A CUCKOO GAME

Tick-Tock

Tick-tock, tick-tock,
swing baby from side to side

I'm a little cuckoo clock.
swing her from side to side

Tick-tock, tick-tock,
swing her from side to side

now I'm striking one o'clock.
lift baby up to the sky gently just once

Cuckoo! Cuckoo!

repeat verses with two and three o'clock, raising her up two and three times, respectively

Balance	✔
Body Awareness	✔
Listening	✔

WITH A SIMPLE CHANT, some soft swaying, and a gentle lift in the air, this activity is sure to please most babies. Hold your baby under her arms and keep her head upright. You can sit or stand with your baby either facing you or out into the room. Babies also like to watch each other doing this activity. So if your little one has a little playmate, let them face each other while the parents sing the song. When your baby gets too heavy for you to lift this way, you can turn the game into a lap ride by chanting the words as you rock back and forth and gently bounce her on your lap.

"Cuckoo! Cuckoo!"

RESEARCH REPORT

You may think *your infant isn't paying attention to music yet. In fact, numerous studies in recent years have shown that babies can remember a melody and comprehend rhythm, and that music even sets off memories for them. In one study of three-month-old babies, researchers played a song while babies played with mobiles. When the babies heard that same song either one day or seven days later, they started inter-acting with their mobiles once again.*

SHE HAS NO IDEA what a clock is, but swinging from side to side is delightful just the same.

JUST OUT OF REACH

MOVEMENT MOTIVATION

SKILL SPOTLIGHT

Even before your baby *can sit up on his own, he may be starting to roll from one side to the other. That means he's beginning to realize that he's a self-propelling creature. Enticing him with interesting-looking objects may encourage his emerging mobility. Accompanying the exercise with playful interactions helps build a close relationship between you and your child and sows the seeds for healthy self-esteem.*

| Gross Motor Skills | ✔ |
| Social Development | ✔ |

YOU CAN ENCOURAGE your baby's early efforts to grab things and even to move his body by placing attractive objects (brightly colored balls, plush toys, favorite picture books, and, most especially, yourself) just beyond his reach. Encourage him to get to the objects in any way he can, whether by creeping forward on his tummy, rolling over on his side, or just plain s-t-r-e-t-c-h-i-n-g as far as he can go. Don't tease him, though. Instead, build success into the activity. If he starts to get frustrated, hand him the toy and praise his efforts.

STRETCHING, ROLLING, and "tummy time" build strength needed for crawling.

BELLY ROLL

BODY AWARENESS FOR BEGINNERS

WHEN HE WAS FIRST BORN, your baby couldn't tell the difference between his being and your being, or where his body ended and yours began. You can boost his budding body awareness and stimulate his little body by gently rolling a small beach ball across his tummy and up and down his legs and arms. Does he want to grab it or kick it? Let him at it — it's excellent coordination practice. You can also try putting him on his tummy and rolling the ball down his back. Singing a song during this activity can add to the fun.

SKILL SPOTLIGHT

The gentle massage *from the ball provides tactile stimulation and helps your baby become aware of his own body. Grasping the ball helps him develop eye-hand coordination. Sitting upright and holding on to the ball with your support will help him learn balance.*

✔ **Balance**

✔ **Body Awareness**

✔ **Tactile Stimulation**

THE TICKLING PRESSURE OF a rolling beach ball helps him learn more about his body.

67

KITCHEN FUN

NOW YOU'RE COOKING

SKILL SPOTLIGHT

As he manipulates *cups and spoons by dropping them, picking them up, and placing them in his mouth, your baby learns about using his arms and hands. Exploring objects by mouth helps your baby learn about physical properties such as smooth, rough, cold, hard, light, and heavy. Your participation in such activities helps ensure your baby's success.*

Eye-Hand Coordination	✔
Fine Motor Skills	✔
Gross Motor Skills	✔

IF YOUR BABY ENJOYS THIS ACTIVITY, also try Swat the Toy, page 49.

JUST BECAUSE YOUR BABY can reach out and grasp something – a rattle, a stuffed animal, or a lock of your hair – doesn't mean he can control that object very well. Becoming truly dexterous requires fine control of the wrist, palm, and fingers, as well as the ability to judge distance and shapes. All that takes plenty of practice. Sets of plastic measuring cups and spoons are great toys at this stage because they're easy to grasp and have interesting surfaces. If your baby has learned to pick up things on his own, just place them around him on the floor. If his aim isn't yet perfected, place the spoons in his hand and encourage him to hold them. Don't be surprised or disappointed if the spoons immediately go in his mouth. Gumming objects is a healthy way for babies to learn about the world.

EXPLORING WITH SPOONS helps him understand how his hands, his arms, and various-sized objects actually work.

RESEARCHREPORT

While there is *a genetic component to the "handedness" (right-handed vs. left-handed) your baby adopts, a mother's style may also have a strong influence. In a study of infant–mother pairs, researchers at DePaul University found that babies often matched their mother's handedness during toy play, and that the matching increased as the baby got older. A father's handedness tends not to have as much of an effect, perhaps because statistically moms spend more time with young babies.*

KNEE RIDES

ADD A LITTLE BOUNCE to lap time by propping up your baby on your knee and gently rocking her back and forth while you sing a children's song. It's a good way for her to gain a sense of rhythm and challenge her sense of balance.

TO MARKET, TO MARKET

To market, to market,
to buy a fat pig,
home again, home again,
jiggety jig.

To market, to market,
to buy a fat hog,
home again, home again,
jiggety jog.

To market, to market,
to buy a plum bun,
home again, home again,
marketing's done.

TROT, TROT, TROT

Trot, trot to London,
rock baby side to side on lap
trot, trot to Dover.
Look out, (baby's name),
or you might fall O-VER.
tip baby to one side

Trot, trot to Boston,
rock baby side to side on lap
trot, trot to Lynn.
support baby's waist and neck
with your hands
Look out, (baby's name),
or you might fall IN!
gently let the baby drop through
the space between your legs

SKIP TO MY LOU

Skip, skip, skip to my Lou,
rock baby rhythmically from side to side
skip, skip, skip to my Lou,
skip, skip, skip to my Lou,
skip to my Lou, my darling.

Lost my partner, what'll I do?
rock baby back and forth
Lost my partner, what'll I do?
Lost my partner, what'll I do?
Skip to my Lou, my darling.

I'll find another one, prettier too,
raise baby up on knees, and down again
I'll find another one, prettier too,
I'll find another one, prettier too,
skip to my Lou, my darling.

Flies in the buttermilk, shoo fly shoo,
rock baby on knee, exaggerate "shoo" sound
flies in the buttermilk, shoo fly shoo,
flies in the buttermilk, shoo fly shoo,
skip to my Lou, my darling.

MY BONNIE

My Bonnie lies over the ocean,
rock baby to left
my Bonnie lies over the sea,
rock baby to right
my Bonnie lies over the ocean,
lean backwards
oh bring back my Bonnie to me.
pull baby tight to chest

Bring back, bring back,
rock baby back and forth
oh bring back my Bonnie
to me, to me.
Bring back, bring back,
rock baby back and forth
oh bring back
my Bonnie to me.
end with a big hug

FEW BABIES can resist a silly song and a rhythmic rock with a parent.

WAY HIGH

EARLY FLIGHT LESSONS

SKILL SPOTLIGHT

Although he's firmly held *by you, this "flying" activity helps him develop the large muscles in his back and shoulders, especially if he lifts his head up to look at the scenery. It also gives him a chance to develop a fledgling sense of balance. You won't let him go, of course, but he'll feel his center of gravity shifting as he "flies" up and down.*

Balance	✔
Upper-Body Strength	✔

If your baby enjoys this activity, also try Airplane Baby, page 32.

YOUR UNCLE may have tossed you in the air when you were young – and you may have loved it – but such baby-as-beach-ball activities are no longer considered safe. You can still have fun "flying" with your baby, however – just be sure to keep a steady grip on his tiny torso and keep your movements gentle. Sit upright with your baby in front of you on the floor. Lift him up in the air, then roll onto your back, lifting him over your head. You can also place his tummy on your shins while you lie back and gently sway or lift your legs while holding his arms. Either way, he will enjoy the feeling of soaring through the air, even while you're safely supporting him. Sing a song like "I'm Flying High" (opposite) to add to his fun.

MOMMY'S STEADY HANDS, happy song, and smiling face make "rough-housing" safe and fun.

72

I'm Flying High

to the *tune* of **"Little Teapot"**

**I'm a little baby,
I fly high.**

**Here is the floor,
here is the sky.**

**Like a little bird
or butterfly.**

**Now UP I go –
I'm flying high.**

73

BABY'S FIRST BOOKS

READY FOR READING

Emotional Development	✔
Language Development	✔
Visual Development	✔

HE'S TOO YOUNG to understand a story line. He's probably too young even to turn the pages. But introducing your young baby to the pleasures of books is one of the best things you can do for him, as it builds a positive association with reading.

• Small, square board books are easiest at this age, as your baby can gum them, swat at them, and grab at them without damaging the pages. In the second half of this first year, when your baby learns to turn his own pages, look for plastic bath books or books with cloth pages, which will be easier for him to handle.

• Books with colorful pictures and a minimum of text are the best choices, as they introduce him to the magic of illustrated worlds without too much narration. Point out the objects in each picture — "See the duck?" "Where are the socks?" Someday soon he'll surprise you by pointing to such objects on his own.

• Most young babies won't sit still for a full narration and instead may enjoy simply exploring the pages. Other babies are lulled by the cadence of nursery rhymes and similar story lines. Your baby knows best what kind of storybook session he likes, so follow his lead.

◀ *IF YOUR BABY ENJOYS THIS ACTIVITY, also try Friendly Faces, page 56.*

RESEARCH REPORT

He can hardly sit up *and he can't tell a chicken from a dump truck. So why read to a baby? Research shows that reading, even to young babies, helps them build their "receptive" vocabularies (the number of words they under- stand). In one study at Rhode Island Hospital, researchers com- pared the receptive vocabularies of two groups of eighteen-month- olds. One group had been read to often as babies; the other had not. The frequent-reading group's vocabulary had increased 40 percent since babyhood; the nonreading group's vocabulary had increased just 16 percent.*

EVEN THE YOUNGEST BABIES enjoy time spent snuggling, listening to words, and looking at colorful pictures.

EYES, NOSE, MOUTH, TOES

A BODY EXERCISE

SKILL SPOTLIGHT

Your young baby *is not going to repeat any of these body-part names; that comes later on. But your touch provides tactile stimulation and helps her become more aware of her body's parameters and movements. Naming body parts often enough eventually will help her to recognize them and learn how to say them herself.*

Body Awareness	✔
Language Development	✔
Tactile Stimulation	✔

◀ *IF YOUR BABY ENJOYS THIS ACTIVITY, also try Babbling With Baby, page 52.*

HER KICKING FEET, waving hands, and general jiggling and giggling are all signs that your baby is beginning to understand that she can somewhat control the movements of her own body. Reinforce this dawning realization by pointing out the major body parts for her. Place her on a bed, carpet, or changing table. Touch her face and say "face." Then place her little hands on your face and repeat "face." Then do her eyes, nose, mouth, and chin, and her legs, tummy, feet, and toes, each time letting her feel both her own body and yours.

"THIS IS YOUR FACE, this is my face." Before you know it, she'll be touching her own face when you say the word.

WHAT'S SQUEAKING?

A HANDS-ON EXERCISE

BETWEEN THE THIRD and fourth months, most babies learn to reach for and grasp objects. This isn't an easy task; it requires your baby to have significant hand control. It's an exciting discovery, however, as he can now draw objects in the world toward himself rather than waiting for you to deliver them. To help him practice, hold two squeaky toys in front of him. Squeezing first one and then the other, encourage him to grab at the toys.

SKILL SPOTLIGHT

At first your baby *may just wave his hands and kick excitedly. But squeaky toys are enticing enough that he'll start swiping at them – which is good practice for his hand-eye coordination and shows him just how far his body reaches. If he makes contact with the toy, let him hold it; the sense of accomplishment and satisfaction he gets will be a reward that inspires him to try this activity again and again.*

| ✔ | **Eye-Hand Coordination** |
| ✔ | **Listening** |

FEW BABIES CAN RESIST the sound and sight of a colorful squeaky toy, especially when both parents join in the fun.

IF YOUR BABY ENJOYS THIS ACTIVITY, also try Big Bouncing Ball, page 80.

BUBBLES FOR BABY

REACHING, TOUCHING, POPPING

SKILL SPOTLIGHT

Watching bubbles float *through the air helps your baby practice his visual skills such as eye tracking, distance, and depth perception. Trying to swat at them is excellent practice for his budding eye-hand coordination. And if he should actually catch one, he'll get a lesson in the relationship between cause (I touch the bubble) and effect (The bubble pops!).*

MAKING YOUR OWN

For the soap solution, mix 1 cup of water, 1 teaspoon of glycerin (available in pharmacies), and 2 tablespoons of dishwashing detergent. Make bubble wands from plastic lids with the center cut out. But be sure to keep these away from your baby.

Cause and Effect	✔
Eye-Hand Coordination	✔
Visual Development	✔

HAS IT BEEN DECADES since you last pondered the magic of iridescent bubbles floating in the air? Don't let that stop you from sharing this simple — and highly entertaining — activity with your baby.

• Buy a variety of bubble-blowing toys, and blow different-sized bubbles for your baby. If you aim large bubbles at a cloth, soft carpet, or bath water, the bubbles will stick longer, which will give five- and six-month-olds a chance to "catch" their first one. Or create a shower of small bubbles by blowing quickly through a wand or pipe. Tracking bubbles in midair hones your baby's developing visual skills.

• A cascade of bubbles makes a pleasant distraction during diaper-changing time. Blowing bubbles while he's bathing will make bath time fun (and the bathtub also helps contain the soapy residue that some bubbles leave on surfaces). Bubbles billowing outside are especially enchanting. Wave the wand way up high, or blow the bubbles low to the ground so they drift skyward on air currents.

IF YOUR BABY ENJOYS THIS ACTIVITY, also try Pinwheel Magic, page 63.

BUBBLES ARE FASCINATING
baubles—even for very young babies.

BIG BOUNCING BALL

SWATTING PRACTICE

SKILLSPOTLIGHT

He can't grab objects *until he can literally learn to aim and fire those little hands and feet. That takes eye-hand and eye-foot co-ordination, as well as an understanding of just how far those arms and legs extend – all of which come from steady swatting and kicking practice.*

Eye-Foot Coordination	✔
Eye-Hand Coordination	✔
Tactile Stimulation	✔
Visual Development	✔

SOMETIMES IT'S THE SIMPLEST TOYS that give a baby the biggest kick for the longest amount of time. For instance, an old-fashioned, brightly colored punchball (available at toy stores) can engage a baby all through the first half of his first year – and even beyond. Newborns will gaze at the orb if it's hung from a ceiling or doorway. Three- to six-month-olds can swat it with their hands, kick it with their feet, and eventually try to get both arms around it. Can't find a punchball? Hang a beach ball instead. Whichever you choose, always supervise your baby with the ball.

HE'LL LOVE SWATTING at this big, colorful ball.

80

JACK-IN-THE-BOX

THE JOY OF SURPRISES

TAKE A GAME OF PEEKABOO, add a little music, throw in the surprise effect of having a toy clown pop out from a box, and you've got the perfect activity for a five- or six-month-old baby. Once she learns that a toy comes out every time, the anticipation will build until it's hard for her to contain her excitement. Soon she'll be helping you stuff the toy back in the box, and waiting expectantly for you to close the lid, turn the handle, and make the clown pop out again.

AFTER THE "POP," she'll help you stuff the clown back in its box.

SKILL SPOTLIGHT

The sound of a crank *going round and round, as well as the delicious "pop" of a toy springing from its box, provide auditory stimulation for your baby. Equally important, the repetition of the toy's appearance and disappearance reinforces her growing understanding of object permanence.*

✔	**Cause & Effect**
✔	**Listening**
✔	**Visual Stimulation**

IF YOUR BABY ENJOYS THIS ACTIVITY, also try Peekaboo Games, page 51.

81

PUSHING GAME

LOWER-BODY EXERCISES

SKILL SPOTLIGHT

A baby's muscles develop *from the head and neck, shoulders, and arms; down the back; and finally to the hips, thighs, and calves. At this age your baby's upper body may be pretty well developed (that's why he can sit up), but his legs aren't quite sturdy enough for him to crawl. This exercise helps strengthen them and also gives him a taste of what it takes to get some forward motion.*

Balance	✔
Gross Motor Skills	✔
Upper-Body Strength	✔

IF YOUR BABY ENJOYS THIS ACTIVITY, also try Just Out of Reach, page 66.

HE THINKS HE CAN, he thinks he can...he thinks he can move forward on his tummy, but he's not quite coordinated enough yet. Give him a boost by laying him on his front and letting him push against your hands or a rolled-up towel with his feet. Don't push, but support his feet with your hands as he inches forward each time. One minute of creeping practice now and again may be exhilarating; two minutes may be all he needs to get moving down the path toward greater mobility.

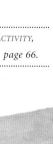

SOMETIMES A LITTLE SUPPORT from behind can help get your budding crawler moving.

SURPRISES INSIDE

6 MONTHS AND UP 6

FINGER FUN AND PAPER MAGIC

H E'S RUMMAGING through the drawers, digging through the magazine rack, and pulling all his books off his shelf. His constant explorations are probably creating chaos in your home, but they're actually a sign of healthy infant development. Here's a way to put those little hands to good, nondestructive use: loosely wrap some of his toys in brightly colored paper, put them all in a big shopping bag, and let him dig through, unwrap, and rediscover his things. This is a great activity during car trips and airplane flights.

IT'S THE SAME BALL he's had for months, but it's a new surprise when he finds it inside brightly colored paper.

SKILLSPOTLIGHT

It takes fine motor skills *to figure out how to unwrap an object, and your baby will delight in the sound of crumpled paper. You may have to show him how to unwrap the objects at first, of course, but once he masters it, he'll soon understand that good things come in wrapped packages.*

✔	**Fine Motor Skills**
✔	**Problem Solving**
✔	**Tactile Stimulation**

IF YOUR BABY ENJOYS THIS ACTIVITY, also try Boxed Set, page 134.

83

SHAKE, RATTLE, AND ROLL

A RATTLE FOR BIG BABIES

SKILL SPOTLIGHT

Mastering the fun shaking *motion and creating the rattling sound will make your baby feel powerful and boost his awareness of cause and effect as he replicates the noise over and over again. It will also help him express his growing sense of rhythm and develop his gross motor skills.*

MAKING YOUR OWN

Plastic spice bottles work well for homemade maracas because they're small enough for your baby to wrap his hands around. Fill them with sand, dried beans, or pebbles; secure the tops firmly with duct tape or glue; and he's ready to shake!

BY SIX MONTHS, your baby has a pretty good sense that his hands are connected to his arms and has pretty good control of the movements of both his arms and hands. Now he wants to use his hands to explore his environment, whether by patting, stroking, or grabbing at nearly everything around him. As he discovers the properties of the objects he touches — their shape, weight, texture, and, of course, taste — he'll be particularly amazed by the various sounds they make. You can help his early experiments by providing a simple maraca made from a plastic bottle filled with something that will make noise. Show him how to shake it — but once he gets the idea, it may be hard to get him to stop!

Cause & Effect	✔
Gross Motor Skills	✔
Listening	✔

IF YOUR BABY ENJOYS THIS ACTIVITY, also try Music Maker, page 92.

6 MONTHS
6
AND UP

"Shake it up, baby!"

A BOTTLE FILLED WITH SAND is a simple toy, but the sound it makes is music to your baby's ears.

DUMPING OUT TOYS is even
more fun with a playmate.

DUMPING DELIGHTS

A PUTTING-IN AND TAKING-OUT GAME

DUMPING THINGS out of containers and then putting them back in again is a favorite sport of babies who have learned to sit up and use their hands. Wherever he is in the house, your baby will probably find something to empty and fill. And while he will be happy to empty out the contents of your wastebaskets or cupboards all morning long, you can let him play a cleaner and more baby-friendly putting-in and taking-out game by giving him a wide-mouthed, gallon-sized plastic jar, a large plastic storage container, or even a large stainless steel bowl of his own. Fill the container with measuring cups, plastic bowls, blocks, small plush toys, plastic rings, and rattles. Then sit alongside him on the floor and help him fill and dump the container a few times. He will soon be busily doing the job on his own – over and over again.

SKILLSPOTLIGHT

Besides entertaining *your baby, dumping and filling containers teaches him about the relative sizes, shapes, and weights of various objects. It also introduces him to spatial concepts such as big and small, and empty and full. Dumping out and putting back exercises both fine and gross motor skills.*

✔	**Fine Motor Skills**
✔	**Gross Motor Skills**
✔	**Size and Shape Discrimination**
✔	**Spatial Awareness**

IF YOUR BABY ENJOYS THIS ACTIVITY, also try Baby's Cupboard, page 108. ▶

BABYPROOFING

WHETHER she's rolling, creeping, crawling, pulling up, or cruising at this stage, a mobile baby is quite capable of harming herself. Some kinds of babyproofing depend on your baby's particular interests (not all babies are fascinated with potted plants, for example). But some kinds need to be done regardless of your baby's current behavior, because the consequences can be dire.

Electrical outlets: Babies are very curious about tiny holes. Outlet covers are easy to install and can avert a possible disaster.

Cupboards: Any cupboard or drawer that contains sharp, poisonous, or breakable objects needs to have a babyproof lock. Better yet, move dangerous items out of your baby's reach.

Unstable furniture: If your baby bangs into or pulls up on a piece of unstable furniture, she could knock it over and injure herself. Bolt unstable furniture (such as bookshelves) to walls and keep heavy objects off furniture that wobbles when touched.

Choking hazards: Keep an eagle eye out for small objects that often fall on the floors of your home, such as buttons, needles, coins, pills, or earrings. Regular sweeping and vacuuming can help keep these hazards to a minimum.

Stairs: Install barriers at the top and bottom of each flight of stairs in your home.

Adult stuff: Be constantly on the lookout to make sure things such as knives, scissors, letter openers, razors, pens, power cords, and glasses stay out of your baby's reach.

Unfortunately, babyproofing is not a one-step operation. As your baby gets older, taller, more mobile, and bolder, you'll need to monitor what she can hit her head on, what she can reach, and what she can put her fingers into. ■

SWITCHING GAME

TAKING TURNS WITH HANDS

BY NOW your baby has a good grasp of getting hold of objects – whether it's her favorite stuffed duck or a lock of your hair. But she may not be quite so adept at passing an object from one hand to another, which involves moving two hands at once. (Instead, she'll probably drop one object when offered another.) To help her practice using both hands, put a small toy in one. Let her play with it for a while, then hold another toy up toward that same hand. Encourage her to switch the first toy from one hand to the other, rather than simply dropping it. Her reward for accomplishing this tricky task? Getting to hold two toys at once!

SKILL SPOTLIGHT

Passing a toy *from one hand to another helps her learn to grasp and release simultaneously – not an easy task for a baby. It will also help her to cross over the vertical midline of her body with her hands, a precursor to crawling and walking.*

✔	**Bilateral Coordination**
✔	**Eye-Hand Coordination**
✔	**Fine Motor Skills**
✔	**Grasp and Release**

HOLDING TWO TOYS at once takes practice, but the result is twice as nice!

89

PLAY BALL

CRAWLING AND CATCHING FUN

SKILLSPOTLIGHT

Having a desirable object *move just beyond reach may inspire your baby to pursue the next mobility task, whether it's rolling, creeping, or crawling. Learning how to stop a moving object reinforces her developing sense of personal power as she exerts control over her environment. But don't expect her to roll or throw the ball back to you; those are skills she develops in her second year.*

Balance	✔
Eye-Hand Coordination	✔
Gross Motor Skills	✔
Spatial Awareness	✔

SHE'S NOT QUITE READY for a game of catch, but a game of fetch will please her no end. Roll a medium-sized whiffle ball, a blown-up beach ball, or a large cloth ball just beyond your baby so that she has to move to get it. Or try rolling it to her directly so that she can get used to stopping it with her hands. Here's a hint: letting a little air out of a big plastic ball or beach ball will make it easier for her to grab and handle.

A BABY WILL DELIGHT in stopping a rolling ball – and learning about objects in motion.

90

"Here comes the ball!"

RESEARCHREPORT

It's one of those days *when you're tired and maybe even a little cross, so you're not quite up to laughing, clapping, and urging your baby on. Can she tell the difference? Studies show that when parents deliberately interact in an emotionally flat way, their babies use facial expressions and vocalizations to try to get them to act "normally" again, evidence that they're seeking to "repair" the interaction. Of course it's OK, and perfectly normal, to have a bad day once in a while. But, if you can respond positively (with a smile and a hug, perhaps), your baby will gain confidence in her ability to regulate social interactions, and it might make you feel better, too.*

6 MONTHS
6
AND UP

MUSIC MAKER

A SOUND BACKGROUND

SKILLSPOTLIGHT

Matching an external beat
isn't a part of her musical skill set yet, but understanding that music is participatory and fun helps both her musical and social development. This activity actually works on both her gross and fine motor skills and sets up a positive association with music.

Fine Motor Skills	✔
Gross Motor Skills	✔
Listening	✔
Rhythm Exploration	✔

◀ *IF YOUR BABY ENJOYS THIS ACTIVITY, also try Shake, Rattle, and Roll, page 84.*

IT'S NEVER TOO EARLY to expose your baby to music, but it's not until she's old enough to control objects (even somewhat) that she can become an active player. You can enhance her listening pleasure by giving her things to shake, rattle, and roll while she listens to music or you singing. Just gather together rattles, squeaky toys, and shakers. Show her how to use them, and then allow her to let loose.

A BABY BECOMES her own rhythm section as soon as she gets some musical toys.

TOTALLY TUBULAR

6 MONTHS AND UP

A STACKING GAME

YOUR BABY may not have entered an ocean, a lake, or even a kiddie pool yet, but swim tubes provide plenty of fun on dry land, too. Sitters and crawlers alike enjoy using the tubes for sitting support. Or play a game of peekaboo in the rings. Just sit her down in one on a soft surface, stack the rest of them up to her chest, and lift them off while calling "Peekaboo!" Babies who are more mobile will take pleasure in creeping and crawling in and out of several tubes placed on the floor.

SKILL SPOTLIGHT

Playing peekaboo with swim tubes lets babies experience a temporary visual separation from you, which will eventually help them understand that even if you leave, you haven't disappeared forever. Crawling in, out, and over the rings lets babies practice being mobile on an uneven surface, which helps them develop balance and coordination.

✔	**Balance**
✔	**Gross Motor Skills**
✔	**Object Permanence**

STACK THEM UP and let the fun begin. You can play all sorts of baby games with a set of swim tubes.

93

CLAPPING SONGS

AS YOUR BABY'S manual dexterity improves, she'll become fascinated with hand movements such as clapping, snapping, and waving. Amplify her delight by singing songs that incorporate simple gestures. While she won't be able to perform each movement right away, eventually she'll learn to clap or wave. Coax her by clapping or waving her hands for her, or clapping and waving yourself.

BINGO

There was a farmer had a dog
and Bingo was his name-o
B-I-N-G-O
B-I-N-G-O
B-I-N-G-O
and Bingo was his name-o.

There was a farmer had a dog
and Bingo was his name-o
clap-I-N-G-O
clap-I-N-G-O
clap-I-N-G-O
and Bingo was his name-o.
keep adding one clap and removing one letter

THIS OLD MAN

clap out rhythm throughout

**This old man, he played one,
he played knick knack on my thumb,
with a knick, knack, paddy whack,
give a dog a bone,
this old man went rolling home.**

**This old man, he played two,
he played knick knack on my shoe,
with a knick, knack, paddy whack,
give a dog a bone,
this old man went rolling home.**

*continue with additional verses:
three/knee, four/door, five/hive,
six/sticks, seven/up in heaven, eight/gate,
nine/spine, ten/once again*

WHETHER YOU'RE MAKING the movement for her or she's making elementary motions herself, putting words, music, and gestures together helps build your baby's vocabulary.

WORKING ON THE RAILROAD

**I've been working on the railroad
all the livelong day.**
make digging motions with hands

**I've been working on the railroad
just to pass the time away.
Can't you hear the whistle blowin'?**
pull an imaginary whistle string

Rise up so early in the morn.
raise hands into air

**Can't you hear the
captain shouting,**
clap

**"Dinah, blow
your horn."**

6 MONTHS AND UP

LITTLE DRUMMER BABY

BANGING AWAY

SKILL SPOTLIGHT

At this age, *babies start to get a very elementary understanding of cause and effect. Hitting an object and having it make noise reinforces that concept while strengthening the baby's eye-hand coordination. And hearing the different sounds that various objects make helps him learn about the properties of those objects, which he'll later transfer to other situations.*

Cause & Effect	✔
Eye-Hand Coordination	✔
Listening	✔

IF YOUR BABY ENJOYS THIS ACTIVITY, also try Music Maker, page 92.

BEING ABLE TO MANIPULATE OBJECTS is very gratifying for young babies who are working on fine motor control; being able to make noises with those objects is even more so. You can entertain your baby by setting pots, pans, and bowls near him and providing him with wooden spoons. Show your baby how to hit the "drums" to make a noise, then encourage him to try it himself. He may hit the pots accidentally, which will give him enough of a taste to start tapping them on purpose.

A RAT-A-TAT-TAT and a sis-boom-bang . . . this elementary drum set introduces him to the joys of noise, as well as to the idea that his actions influence his world.

FINGERPUPPET FUN

MAGIC AT YOUR FINGERTIPS

MESMERIZED BY MOTION and enchanted by animal toys, babies are natural audiences for a miniature puppet show. Just slip on a fingerpuppet or two and let them bob, dance, kiss, tickle, sing, and talk to your littlest spectator. At this age, he's likely to reach out, grab a puppet, and start to mouth it. This is fine as long as the puppets have no small parts that can be pulled off and swallowed. He's equally likely to babble, gurgle, and blow raspberries at the animated actors. You can also find a song to go with your fingerpuppets and make it a musical show!

SKILL SPOTLIGHT

Listening to the puppets *talk and sing will help him learn the art of conversation – that is, that first one person (or puppet, as the case may be) talks, and then the other person responds. Being tickled and nuzzled by his little friends provides both entertaining tactile stimulation and fun, positive interaction with you.*

✔ **Social Development**

✔ **Tactile Stimulation**

A PERKY PURPLE MOUSE gives him someone new to babble with.

97

"Where's the scarf?"

SOMETIMES IT TAKES nothing more than
a cardboard tube, a colorful scarf, and
Mommy's time to put a baby on cloud nine.

MAGIC SCARVES

A REAPPEARING ACT

IF YOU'RE LOOKING for a versatile toy that will last through several of your child's developmental stages, you need look no further than your own clothes closet. Silky scarves can delight and entertain him up through his preschool years. When he's still a baby, one of the best games you can play is to poke a brightly colored scarf through one end of a cardboard tube and let him pull it out the other side. You can play the game without the tube by hiding most of the scarf in your fist and letting him find and grab the end. Embellish the game by adding your own enticements — "Where's the scarf? Where did it go? Oh, there it is! Peekaboo!" — to help keep him engaged.

MAKING YOUR OWN

If you don't have any scarves, you can buy colorful squares of cloth at fabric or novelty stores. For a change, use an empty tissue box instead of the cardboard tube—show your baby how to stuff the scarf in and pull it out.

SKILLSPOTLIGHT

Grabbing the silky scarf *and pulling it from the tube lets your baby work on his eye-hand coordination along with his fine motor skills. And seeing the scarf first disappear and then reappear at the other end will boost your baby's understanding of object permanence.*

✔	**Eye-Hand Coordination**
✔	**Object Permanence**
✔	**Tactile Stimulation**

IF YOUR BABY ENJOYS THIS ACTIVITY, also try Busy Boxes, page 101. ▶

STOP THE TOP

FUN WITH SPINNING

SKILL SPOTLIGHT

Touching an object *that's just lying there, like a block, is one challenge. Tracking and touching an object that's moving is a completely different challenge – one that this activity lets your baby practice over and over again. In addition, seeing how a gentle touch can either stop the spinning top or send it careening across the floor teaches your baby valuable lessons about cause and effect.*

Cause & Effect	✔
Eye-Hand Coordination	✔
Spatial Awareness	✔

A **SPINNING TOP** is one of those old-fashioned toys that can delight all kinds of babies. Small babies obviously can't pump the handle up and down, but that doesn't mean they have to be passive observers. Instead, make the top spin in front of your baby. Then show him how to stop it by touching it with your hand. He'll soon start reaching out to control the whirling colors and whirring noises himself.

ENCHANT YOUR CHILD with the dazzling colors of a spinning top.

BUSY BOXES

LITTLE TASKS FOR LITTLE FINGERS

ACTIVITY BOARDS with cylinders that whirl, dials that spin, and buttons that squeak can provide hours of amusement for your baby's curious fingers. Just set up the board so she can reach all the stations, and show her how it works. Then let her try her own hand at it. At first, she may only be able to do the very simplest activities on the board, like swatting a rolling ball or sticking her finger in a hole on the dial. In the months to come, though, she'll learn to spin the dial and press the buttons.

YOU'LL PIQUE her curiosity and keep her fingers busy with one of these classic baby toys.

SKILL SPOTLIGHT

Even the simplest activities *help a baby develop finger dexterity and coordination, which leads to more advanced tasks in later months. Learning that touching different knobs creates different results helps her mentally classify those results, and also builds upon her sense of mastery.*

✔	**Cause & Effect**
✔	**Eye-Hand Coordination**
✔	**Fine Motor Skills**

IF YOUR BABY ENJOYS THIS ACTIVITY, also try Activity Book, page 128.

101

SEPARATION ANXIETY

JUST WHEN your baby is gaining a good deal of mobility and a tiny bit of independence, he suddenly wants to be joined to your hip once again. Your baby's newfound independence and his newly expressed separation anxiety are related. Now that he's mobile, he understands how easily the two of you can become separated.

Knowing that your presence means so much can feel flattering, but it can also fray your nerves. Here are some tips to get through this challenging period.

Respect him: Remember that your presence is still essential to your baby, and he can't help being distraught at the thought that you're not there.

Reassure him: Hold him, talk to him, sing to him, and, once he calms down, distract him by giving him a book or toy. Reassurance now will help him feel more secure later.

Protect him: Separation anxiety and stranger anxiety often arrive hand in hand. If strangers get too close, explain that your baby's not comfortable around new people and let him hide on your shoulder. Don't scold him for being shy; he can't help it. Given time, most babies will warm up to new people who are friendly and gentle in their approach.

Tell him the truth: It's tempting to try to slip out the back door when you have to leave him with a caregiver, but that won't help your baby. If he thinks that you really do suddenly disappear from time to time, he's more likely to panic if you step out of the room. Be cheerful and clear when you announce your departure, tell him you love him, and walk out the door. If he learns that he can trust you to be truthful and that you really will return, he'll feel more confident.

Remember, it's not forever: Infants, toddlers, and preschoolers all go through stages of separation anxiety. Given comfort, love, and encouragement, most children become quite independent over time. ■

ROLY-POLY

PULL-UP PRACTICE

YOUR BABY has probably enjoyed rocking and even standing supported in your lap since she was just a few months old. Now that her muscles are getting stronger, she'll be even more motivated to stand on her own two feet with your assistance. Make practice fun by accompanying it with a merry movement chant. Start by laying your baby down on her back so that she's facing you with her legs out straight. Then gently help her to sit and stand as you engage in this roly-poly activity.

SHE'S STANDING, she's learning words, and, best of all, you and she are looking right at each other as you play.

Roly-Poly

Roly-poly, roly-poly,
circle arms around one another
(repeat whenever singing roly-poly)
out, out, out.
move hands away from each other
Roly-poly, roly-poly,
in, in, in.
bring hands together
Roly-poly, roly-poly,
touch your nose.
touch baby's nose
Roly-poly, roly-poly,
touch your toes.
pull baby to seated position
Roly-poly, roly-poly,
up to sky.
pull baby up to standing
Roly-poly, roly-poly,
fly, fly, fly.
lift baby up into the air

✔	**Gross Motor Skills**
✔	**Language Development**
✔	**Lower-Body Strength**

103

LITTLE FOLKS' SONGS

SURE, children's television programs and videos provide lots of new songs for little kids. But sometimes it's the old songs that have the most charm, as they help knit the generations together. Engage your child by singing these songs with our suggested hand gestures, and invite the whole family to join in!

DAISY, DAISY

Daisy, Daisy,
give me your answer, do.
clap hands together

I'm half-crazy
over the love of you.
put hands on baby's cheeks

It won't be a fancy marriage –
I can't afford a carriage.
shrug shoulders with hands turned up

But you'll look sweet upon the seat
point at baby

of a bicycle built for two.
hug baby

IT'S RAINING, IT'S POURING

It's raining, it's pouring,
the old man is snoring.
He bumped his head,
and fell out of bed,
and couldn't get up
in the morning.

RAIN, RAIN, GO AWAY

Rain, rain, go away,
come again some other day.
Rain, rain, go away,
all the children want to play.

POLLY WOLLY DOODLE

**Oh I went down South for
to see my Sal,
sing Polly Wolly Doodle all the day.**
tickle baby under chin or ribs

**My Sal she is a spunky gal,
sing Polly Wolly Doodle all the day.**
tickle baby under chin or ribs

Fare thee well,
wave bye-bye

fare thee well,
wave bye-bye

fare thee well my fairy Faye.
wave bye-bye

For I'm going to Louisiana
run fingers up and down baby's body

**for to see my Susyanna,
sing Polly Wolly Doodle all the day.**
tickle baby under ribs

HEY DIDDLE DIDDLE

**Hey diddle diddle, the cat and
the fiddle,**
make fiddling motion with hands

the cow jumped over the moon.
sail hand through the air

**The little dog laughed to see
such sport**
put hands over eyes

**and the dish ran away
with the spoon.**
run fingers from baby's belly to chin

MOMMY'S LAP is the perfect
place to perch while listening
to favorite songs.

NOW IT'S HERE, now it's gone . . . even a blanket and a toy can teach little ones important lessons about object permanence — and fun.

RESEARCH REPORT

Only a few short months ago, *your baby was still experiencing the jerks, twitches, and funny mouth movements associated with newborn reflexes. Now she's sitting up, kicking her legs, and yanking a blanket off her plush toy. What happened? Those first reflexes, like breathing and the heartbeat, originated in your baby's brain stem, which is fully mature at birth. But between four and seven months, her cortex, which governs motor movements, develops and allows motor skills to blossom.*

WHERE'S THE TOY?

6 MONTHS AND UP

MORE PEEKABOO PLAY

WHEN SHE WAS A NEWBORN, your baby was very much an "out of sight, out of mind" type of creature. That is, if you hid a toy from her, she figured it no longer existed. But now that she's reached the six-month threshold, she's on to better ideas. While she may not know exactly where the toy went or why it disappeared, she does understand that it still exists, somewhere, at least for a little while. You can bolster her understanding of this very basic fact by playing peekaboo games with toys.

• Partially hide a favorite plush toy or book under one of her blankets. Ask her repeatedly, "Where is it?" She may need some help finding it the first time, but once she realizes that the rest of the toy is connected to the part that's showing, she'll be diving under the blanket with joy.

• Soon you can begin hiding the toy completely. As long as your baby sees you hide it or notices the toy's outline beneath the blanket, she should be able to find it.

IF YOUR BABY ENJOYS THIS ACTIVITY, also try Peekaboo Games, page 51.

SKILL SPOTLIGHT

Learning that something *exists even when she can't see it helps your baby understand object permanence. This is key to her ability to tolerate separations from you, as well as to remember people, places, or objects she saw previously but that are currently out of sight. This ability is called "representational memory."*

✔ **Fine Motor Skills**

✔ **Object Permanence**

BABY'S CUPBOARD

EARLY EXPLORATIONS

SKILLSPOTLIGHT

Shelves filled *with tempting "toys" help your baby practice her "aim and fire" technique – that is, her ability to see an object, reach for it, and grab it. Having a variety of objects to manipulate lets your baby learn about physical properties such as size, shape, and weight. It also gives her a chance to explore and discover safe items on her own terms.*

Fine Motor Skills	✔
Gross Motor Skills	✔
Sensory Development	✔
Visual Discrimination	✔

NOW THAT YOUR BABY'S getting mobile, it's crucial that you babyproof any cupboards containing breakables, cleaning products, heavy pots and pans, or other materials that could harm her. But if she sees you taking things out of cupboards, it's guaranteed she'll want to do the same – grabbing games, like clearing shelves and emptying cupboards, are favorite pastimes of babies this age. You can keep your baby safe and satisfy her urge to explore and imitate by devoting a cupboard especially to her. An unlocked cabinet stocked with safe, appealing objects like towels, plastic bowls, measuring cups, muffin tins, and a few favorite toys will keep her happily occupied – and it will give you some time to focus on cooking, washing dishes, or even reading the newspaper!

IF YOUR BABY ENJOYS THIS ACTIVITY, also try Dumping Delights, page 86.

BABY'S "WORKING" in the kitchen just like you, but she's not getting into trouble, or even making a mess!

I'M GONNA GET YOU

AN OLD-FASHIONED GAME OF CHASE

SKILLSPOTLIGHT

This is a game *for two to play, and it can help build your baby's social awareness as well as his sense of trust. Having an incentive to crawl also strengthens his balance and gross motor skills.*

Balance	✔
Gross Motor Skills	✔
Social Development	✔
Trust	✔

NO ONE REALLY KNOWS why babies love to be chased and surprised. Whatever the reason, even most early crawlers seem to think that having a beloved caretaker thundering along after them is very, very funny.

• Start crawling slowly after your baby, murmuring "I'm gonna get you …I'm gonna get you …I'm gonna get you!" Then gently grab your baby and say, "I got you!" You can lift him up in the air, kiss the nape of his neck, and give his ribs a little tickle, but keep the game gentle so you don't startle him — he's still a baby, after all.

• A good game of chase isn't just for crawlers; it will keep him on his toes as a toddler and eventually evolve into classic big-kid games like hide-and-seek and tag.

A GENTLE GAME OF CHASE teaches him that Mom can be fun and boisterous as well as cuddly and calm. This helps him understand the range of social behavior humans can show.

110

"I got you!"

RESEARCH REPORT

You may have noticed *that you don't have to start a full-blown game of chase to make your baby squeal with delight. In fact, just the beginning of your special "I'm gonna get you" growly voice can make him giggle. That's because even at this age his memory has developed enough for him to remember what's coming next.*

Does that mean he'll remember your excellent chase style when he's a teenager? That's debatable. For years researchers have believed that events experienced before the development of language couldn't be accessed. But recent research has shown that one- and two-year-olds can recall events from the first year if they're elicited correctly. That means that as a toddler, at least, your child may still appreciate your earlier efforts, even if he can't verbally describe them.

6 MONTHS
6
AND UP

BOTTLE ROLL

GIVING CHASE

SKILLSPOTLIGHT

Encouraging your baby *to grab a rolling bottle will likely motivate him to crawl after it, thereby exercising his gross motor skills. If he prefers to just sit and roll the bottle back and forth, he'll still be working on his fine motor skills as well as his eye-hand coordination.*

Eye-Hand Coordination	✔
Fine Motor Skills	✔
Gross Motor Skills	✔

◀ *IF YOUR BABY ENJOYS THIS ACTIVITY,*
also try Play Ball, page 90.

IT'S OK if your baby starts crawling later than the baby next door – they'll both be running and climbing with abandon in just a few short years. But if you'd like to coax a late or not very enthusiastic crawler into moving a bit more, a baby bottle filled with beans or grains can be an enticing lure. Just fill the bottle partially (so the contents can move) and roll it across the floor in front of your baby. Make sure the bottle top is safely secured. He still won't budge? Show him how to roll it back and forth himself, so he sees that it can provide plenty of sitting entertainment.

GO GET 'EM! He'll love to watch, listen to, and chase after these rolling bottles.

HOW PUZZLING!

FINDING THE RIGHT FIT

ASSEMBLING A JIGSAW PUZZLE is beyond your baby's reach, but she can easily grasp the concept behind the simple wooden puzzles made for older babies and toddlers. Those that feature simple shapes and large pieces with knobs are especially easy, as are those that have matching pictures underneath. There's a knack to getting even these big puzzle pieces in their places, however— you will probably need to guide the pieces as she moves them, so she can feel how they slip into place.

BIG WOODEN PUZZLE PIECES with colorful pictures are pleasing to the eye and help a baby learn about shapes and sizes.

SKILL SPOTLIGHT

Playing with a puzzle – *even getting the pieces out – is great exercise for a baby's fine motor and spatial skills. And learning which piece goes where draws on both her visual memory and her understanding of shapes, sizes, and colors.*

✔	**Fine Motor Skills**
✔	**Problem Solving**
✔	**Size & Shape Discrimination**
✔	**Visual Discrimination**

IF YOUR BABY ENJOYS THIS ACTIVITY, also try Boxed Set, page 134.

113

SOUND STAGE

A LISTENING EXERCISE

SKILLSPOTLIGHT

Focused listening *builds the foundation for your child's language development. It allows him to locate and recognize sounds, and, when combined with other experiences and repetition, allows him to begin forming a repertoire of receptive language.*

Language Development	✔
Listening	✔
Sensory Development	✔
Social Skills	✔

NOT ALL OF YOUR TIME with your baby needs to be spent talking, playing, reading, or otherwise stimulating his little mind. Just sitting and observing the obvious can also build sensory and cognitive awareness. One listening exercise, for instance, is as simple as finding an area where your baby can hear a number of different sounds. It may be inside, where he can hear the dog's toenails clicking on the kitchen floor, the refrigerator running, the telephone ringing, or cars zooming by. Or it may be outside, where he can hear birds singing, leaves rustling, a wind chime jingling, or an airplane overhead. Call his attention to the sounds, point in the right direction, and tell him what they are. You can let him participate in the sounds by hitting the wind chimes, or show him how to imitate the sounds — the "tweet-tweet" of a bird, for instance, or the "vrooom" of a car driving by the house.

IF YOUR BABY ENJOYS THIS ACTIVITY, also try Let's Explore, page 118.

THE SIMPLE SOUNDS of daily life can
be music to the ears of your young one.

115

TRAVELING WITH BABY

BY THE TIME your child is nine months old, life at home has probably settled a bit. You've bonded with your baby, your home is somewhat childproof, and you know how to keep him entertained and safe throughout the day.

But once you leave the comforts of home, life with a baby this age can be unsettling. While a very young baby can sleep through plane changes and family reunions, an older baby has more distinct wants and needs and is less likely to go with the flow.

Does that mean you should avoid travel until your baby is an adolescent? Not at all. Families need to take vacations, and most relatives will relish a visit from you. The trick is to expect the best outcomes but plan for potential obstacles.

Remember his schedule: Planning your travel schedule around your baby's sleep times can help you avoid the stress of dealing with a tired baby once you reach your destination. Throughout your trip, remember that the more rested he is, the more fun your whole family will have.

Remember his important items: If your baby has a stuffed toy or blanket that he uses for comfort, be sure to bring it. Familiar things help to ease the transition to a new environment.

Remember his food: In a hotel or a friend's kitchen, it won't be as easy to whip up his favorite snack. Carry foods like crackers, dry cereal, and fruit, and do a quick shopping trip when you arrive so that you have the food you need on hand.

Remember to babyproof: You won't be able to relax if you're worried about his safety. If you pack a few outlet covers and cupboard locks, you won't need to worry.

Remember your needs: Travel is tiring even when you don't have a baby. Try to eat and sleep well and get some exercise. You can get precious time to yourself by asking a relative to watch your child or by hiring a recommended sitter. ∎

RIDING HIGH

EXPLORING MOVEMENT

SOMETIMES it's hard to know just when to introduce certain toys, because it's hard to know how skilled a baby needs to be to use them. But even a baby who isn't yet walking can use a riding toy, provided her legs are long enough to reach the ground. At first you may have to push her a bit so she understands what this game is all about. But soon she'll be pushing herself along (although, as with crawling, she may go backward at first), and squealing delightedly as she rolls from room to room.

HER FIRST RIDING TOY acquaints her with the delights of independent mobility — and riding it is really good exercise!

SKILL SPOTLIGHT

Most babies won't figure out how to use their legs alternately on a riding toy until their second year. But as they move themselves forward and backward with both feet at once, they'll build strong gross motor skills and improve their balance.

✔	**Balance**
✔	**Gross Motor Skills**
✔	**Lower-Body Strength**

IF YOUR BABY ENJOYS THIS ACTIVITY, also try Push Me, Pull You, page 140.

117

LET'S EXPLORE

BABY'S FIRST TOUR

SKILLSPOTLIGHT

It's easy for adults *to take the daily environment for granted. After all, we've been seeing and hearing it every day for years. But babies are greatly intrigued – and their brains stimulated – by new sights and sounds, and just about everything in your world is still new to them. Encouraging babies to explore the world with their senses, even if it's from the safety of your arms, helps teach them to be actively curious. Your narration also helps your baby build her vocabulary.*

Eye-Hand Coordination	✔
Listening	✔
Sensory Development	✔
Visual Development	✔

AT THIS AGE, your baby's curiosity about the world far exceeds her ability to explore it — even if she is already walking. Give her a lift toward making her first great discoveries by taking her around and describing the local sights.

• Inside the house, show her paintings, posters, books, knobs, and light switches. Let her work the light switch, pull a towel off the rack, or grab a toothbrush from its holder. Describe what she sees and touches — the nubby peel of an orange, for instance, or the soft towel in her hand.

• Take her outside and let her feel the bark of a tree, the leaves on a shrub, or the warmth of a stone in the sun. Lift her up to smell the blossoms on an apple tree or to meet a kitten by the window.

• Don't be surprised if something odd catches her fancy. Most children like animals, but during this stage they also have an interest in inanimate objects such as door hinges, stereo knobs, and push buttons, and are curious about how they work.

◀ *IF YOUR BABY ENJOYS THIS ACTIVITY, also try Sound Stage, page 114.*

SHOWING HER THE MANY different objects in our world and describing them introduces her to important textures, words, and concepts.

SEARCHLIGHT

CATCH THE SPOT

SKILLSPOTLIGHT

Whether your baby *is crawling or walking, trying to catch the colored light improves his eye-hand coordination and agility. Walkers who chase after the beam of light also hone their balance and visual skills.*

Balance	✔
Eye-Hand Coordination	✔
Gross Motor Skills	✔

INCREASED MOBILITY brings with it a whole new range of games that involve chasing and catching. Most of those games have you pursuing your baby. But he can play the pursuer when you show him how to "catch" a flashlight beam. Wrap and secure a layer of tissue paper around the end of a flashlight. Shine the colored light on the floor, on the wall, and on furniture, and encourage your baby to go get it.

FOLLOWING THE CIRCLE of colorful light requires concentration and co-ordination.

OBSTACLE COURSE

A MOBILE PURSUIT

WALKING ON A FLAT SURFACE is one challenge; crawling around or stepping over things while upright is another – and it's an important skill for a baby who's learning to maneuver through a sandbox, around pets, or over the roots of a tree. Help your baby learn to navigate around objects on the ground by setting up a series of small blocks, boxes, and plush toys. If she's walking, hold her hands and help her step over the objects. If she's crawling, encourage her to crawl around this makeshift obstacle course.

MASTERING the challenge of stepping over objects can boost her self-esteem and walking skills.

SKILLSPOTLIGHT

Whether your child *is crawling or already tottering along without holding on, this game helps her learn how to keep her balance. It also helps her develop eye-foot coordination as she practices lifting her feet and putting them in a "safe" spot.*

✔ **Balance**

✔ **Eye-Foot Coordination**

✔ **Gross Motor Skills**

✔ **Lower-Body Strength**

IF YOUR BABY ENJOYS THIS ACTIVITY, also try Upstairs, Downstairs, page 143.

I CAN DO IT, TOO!

COPYCAT FUN

SKILLSPOTLIGHT

Learning how *to put a plush toy in a stroller, how to handle a broom, and how to stir with a plastic spoon helps your baby gain a better sense of spatial relations and develops her fine motor skills. Equally important is the opportunity to mimic what the big kids and adults in her world are doing.*

Fine Motor Skills	✔
Social Skills	✔
Spatial Awareness	✔

AT NINE MONTHS, your baby may already be imitating you by swiping at the floor when you're cleaning or by waving a wooden spoon at a bowl as you cook. Encourage her interest in the adult world by giving her baby-sized versions of brooms, mops, toolboxes, shopping carts, and strollers. If she's walking, you can show her how to take the stuffed dog for a stroller ride. She may not have great coordination at this age, but these are her very first explorations of what will become pretend play, a realm that will engage her increasingly in her toddler and preschool years.

NOTHING IS MORE compelling than doing what big brother does.

122

ZANY XYLOPHONES

SOUNDS OF MUSIC

YOUR BABY'S MUSICAL PURSUITS needn't be limited to baby stuff like rattles, bells, and windup toys. A xylophone designed for children under three years of age (available in music and toy stores) allows her to bang out a tune no matter where the mallet lands. It can also introduce her to the idea of musical scales if you show her how the notes go higher and lower when you play in different directions.

SKILLSPOTLIGHT

Learning how to hear *different notes, and eventually to associate them with different keys, helps your baby develop her listening skills. Gaining the skill to hit the bars one by one helps her develop eye-hand coordination and fine motor skills. And learning that she, too, can make music builds self-esteem.*

✔ **Eye-Hand Coordination**

✔ **Fine Motor Skills**

✔ **Listening**

YOUR BABY WILL LOVE to discover that different colored xylophone bars make different sounds.

◀ IF YOUR BABY ENJOYS THIS ACTIVITY, *also try Music Maker, page 92.*

123

POURING PRACTICE

FILLING FUN

SKILLSPOTLIGHT

When your baby *was younger, he didn't have the coordination to handle most objects. Now he's capable not only of lifting objects but also of tipping and twisting them. This game helps him work with his hands to develop fine motor skills. It also helps him practice his eye-hand coordination.*

Eye-Hand Coordination ✔

Fine Motor Skills ✔

EMPTYING AND FILLING one container is fun; emptying stuff from one container into another is twice as much fun. It's also an easy game to set up. Just gather some plastic cups, bowls, and buckets, plus spoons or small shovels. Then add either water (in a small basin or in the tub), sand (in the sandbox), or cornmeal (at the kitchen table or in a high chair). Show your baby how you fill the cup, spoon, shovel, or bowl with one of the substances. Watch as he enjoys fingering the sand or cornmeal or splashing the water—exploring the textures and how the items work together. Then show your baby how to pour the sand, cornmeal, or water out again. Before long he'll figure out how first to fill a container, then empty it into another.

If your baby enjoys this activity, also try Sand Skills, page 192.

9 MONTHS AND UP

"There it goes!"

A STREAM OF SAND is fascinating to watch and also teaches babies the concepts of empty, full, fast, and slow.

125

ANIMAL SONGS

AT THIS AGE, most babies are beginning to notice the noises animals make and the ways they move. That means it's a good age to introduce songs with funny animal sounds. Your baby will be intrigued by the words and melodies that will later become part of his regular repertoire.

WHERE, OH WHERE

**Oh where, oh where
has my little dog gone?
Oh where, oh where can he be?
With his ears so short
and his tail so long,
oh where, oh where can he be?**

YOUR BABY WILL LOVE interacting with animal puppets as you sing silly animal songs.

SING A SONG OF SIXPENCE

Sing a song of sixpence,
a pocket full of rye,
four and twenty blackbirds,
baked in a pie.

When the pie was opened,
the birds began to sing.
Wasn't that a dainty dish
to set before the king?

OLD MACDONALD

Old MacDonald had a farm,
eee-i-eee-i-o.
And on his farm he had a dog,
eee-i-eee-i-o.
With a woof-woof here
and a woof-woof there,
here a woof, there a woof,
everywhere a woof-woof.
Old MacDonald had a farm,
eee-i-eee-i-o.

continue the song, substituting other
animals and the sounds they make

MARY HAD A LITTLE LAMB

Mary had a little lamb,
little lamb, little lamb,
Mary had a little lamb
whose fleece was white as snow.

Everywhere that Mary went,
Mary went, Mary went,
everywhere that Mary went,
that lamb was sure to go.

ACTIVITY BOOK

THINGS TO SEE AND DO

SKILL SPOTLIGHT

A book with cards to open, textures to feel, and pictures to peruse boosts your baby's budding fine motor skills. Your narration as she looks at the book – "There's the kitty," "This is soft," or "Can you open this?" – helps her learn both words and concepts.

Fine Motor Control	✔
Language Development	✔
Tactile Stimulation	✔

◀ IF YOUR BABY ENJOYS THIS ACTIVITY, also try Friendly Faces, page 56.

IS SHE TURNING book pages, fiddling with clothing labels, and pulling the ties off the tie rack? You can appeal to your baby's tinkering instinct by buying her an activity book or creating one from things found around your house. Just gather together pictures to look at (from magazines and postcards), textures to pat (cotton balls, fake fur, corduroy, crinkly tin foil, or bubble wrap), ribbons to tug, and old cards to open. You can securely glue them to pieces of cardboard and bind it all together with short pieces of ribbon.

YOUR BABY'S MANUAL DEXTERITY, word recognition, and social skills all blossom when two play this game.

KNOCKDOWN

9 MONTHS AND UP

CREATING TOWERS

AS OLDER BABIES gain greater hand and arm coordination, they often take great joy in placing one object on top of another. You can nurture this budding talent by building towers of large blocks, books, cereal boxes, shoe boxes, or plastic bowls and cups for your baby. Remember there are two steps to this fun for your baby: watching you stack the objects and then knocking them down herself.

KNOCKING DOWN the tower is only part of the experience. She is also learning about sizes and shapes.

SKILL SPOTLIGHT

Playing with towers *of toys helps babies develop both gross and fine motor skills. Your baby also has the opportunity to explore spatial relationships and differences in size and shape.*

✔ **Fine Motor Skills**

✔ **Gross Motor Skills**

✔ **Size & Shape Discrimination**

IF YOUR BABY ENJOYS THIS ACTIVITY, also try Boxed Set, page 134. ▶

129

BRIGHT COLORS, easy-to-handle rings, and some simple problems to solve keep babies motivated to stack the large rings again and again.

"Stack them up!"

STACKING RINGS

LEARNING ABOUT SIZE

SOME TOYS never go out of style. Good old-fashioned stacking rings are just as intriguing to babies today as they were to babies generations ago. You can buy sets made of wood or plastic, or make your own. A large set – made of bulky plastic rings, for instance – is usually easiest; older babies, with more advanced fine motor control, can tackle the sets with smaller poles.

• Start by showing your baby how to take the rings off – that's easier than fitting the rings over the pole. Don't be surprised if he just picks up the toy, turns it upside down, and dumps the rings all over the floor. He's showing you the most obvious solution to the problem!

• Learning to stack the rings according to size – with the large ring on the bottom and the small ring on top – comes much later in the second year. In the meantime, just let him practice getting the rings off and on the pole in any order.

MAKING YOUR OWN

As an alternative to a premade stacking ring, take the cardboard tube from a roll of paper towels and some Mason jar rings – or even rings cut from cardboard – and show your baby how to slide them on and off the tube.

SKILL SPOTLIGHT

Figuring out *how to get the colorful rings off – even if it's by dumping them all on the ground at once – helps your child build problem-solving skills. And learning how to place the rings over the pole helps him build both fine motor skills and an understanding of the concept of size.*

✔	**Eye-Hand Coordination**
✔	**Fine Motor Skills**
✔	**Problem Solving**
✔	**Size & Shape Discrimination**

IF YOUR BABY ENJOYS THIS ACTIVITY, also try Knockdown, page 129.

PUBLIC ETIQUETTE

YOUR BABY won't always smile and coo in public — even the happiest baby falls prey to fussiness. And the public won't always be receptive to a fussy baby. But you and your baby have to travel in public, even if it's just for a quick trip to the post office. Your life will be far easier if you learn how to cope with potential conflicts early on.

Countdown to meltdowns: A sure way to create a frustrated, crying baby is to haul her from place to place when she's tired, hungry, or sick. Solution? Don't do it. Try to keep errands short; do them when your baby is rested and well fed; and bring a supply of books and toys for her to play with if you get stuck in a line or traffic jam.

Safeguard your privacy: Even mothers who felt perfectly comfortable nursing their newborn in public may feel a little bashful nursing an eleven-month-old in a shopping mall, especially if that eleven-month-old is walking and starting to talk. Strangers may give you funny looks for "still" nursing such a big baby. If this makes you uncomfortable and you find you have to breast-feed in public, try to find a private corner where you and your baby can be alone and have some quiet time together.

Protect against verbal assault: Blunt remarks about your baby can be annoying and hurtful. The best solution is for you to tactfully respond in a positive way. If someone at the grocery store declares that your baby boy is fat or mistakes him for a girl, you can reply with a very matter-of-fact "Yes, isn't he a gorgeous big boy?"

Part of the art of dealing with awkward situations in public is displaying model behavior for your baby. While he's not old enough to say "Please don't touch me" or "I'll outgrow my baby fat," he is old enough to perceive how you deal with potential conflicts. Staying calm, matter-of-fact, and loving will teach him to behave the same way. ▪

UH-OH!

LEARNING ABOUT CAUSE AND EFFECT

I T'S A SIMPLE FACT that most older babies love to throw things from a higher perch – their highchair, Grandma's lap, etc. Grownups can make this habit into a fun game by engaging the child when she is doing so. Place plastic cups, rattles, large blocks, or small plush toys on the high-chair tray. Then sit on the floor next to the highchair and have the baby hand or toss the toys down to you. You can add to the fun by singing "uh-oh!" or "there it goes," or talking about how the toys go "down" and "up."

SKILLSPOTLIGHT

Dropping and watching *things fall helps a baby learn about cause and effect. At this stage, your baby is also just beginning to understand that through her actions she can exert control over others – something she will test more and more as she gets older.*

✔	**Cause & Effect**
✔	**Eye-Hand Coordination**
✔	**Grasp & Release**
✔	**Social Development**

YOU CAN TURN her natural instinct to throw things into a fun learning game.

133

BOXED SET

OPENING, CLOSING, FILLING, AND EMPTYING

SKILLSPOTLIGHT

A box and a lid *provide an elementary puzzle for a baby, as she has to figure out how to get the lid off (easy) and how to put it back on (harder). This involves coordination and understanding the nature of both shapes and sizes. The activity also introduces her to the concepts of open, shut, full, empty, in, and out.*

Fine Motor Skills	✔
Problem Solving	✔
Size & Shape Discrimination	✔
Spatial Awareness	✔

A **BOX OF WIPES,** a bag of lentils, even the bowl of spaghetti left on the fridge's bottom shelf all fascinate your baby now. She wants to investigate everything in sight. You can safely keep her fingers busy by gathering a set of boxes with easy-to-manage tops (such as shoe boxes, empty diaper-wipe containers, and square gift boxes) and putting small toys and objects inside each.

• Put the same toys in the same boxes every time you play this game.

• Say the words "open" and "closed" as she plays with the boxes, as well as words like "in" and "out" as she plays with the toys.

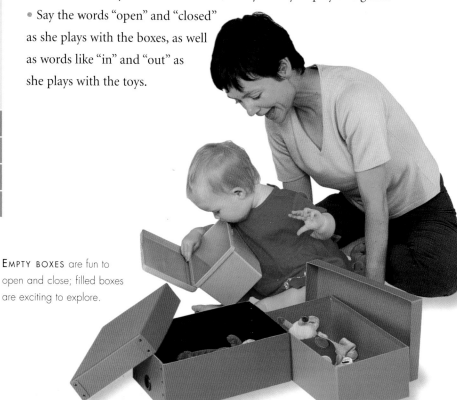

EMPTY BOXES are fun to open and close; filled boxes are exciting to explore.

BALL DROP

AN EYE-HAND COORDINATION EXERCISE

BALLS, BOWLS, and anything that bangs are big, big hits with older babies. How can you incorporate all those elements into one playtime? Just provide your baby with some lightweight balls (like whiffle or tennis balls) and a big metal bowl or plastic basket. Then show your baby how to drop the balls into the container. When the balls hit, they each make an interesting sound. Your baby will be intrigued by this activity and will gain an understanding of cause and effect.

DROPPING A BALL into a large bowl makes a great noise and improves eye-hand coordination.

SKILLSPOTLIGHT

Grabbing a ball *comes pretty naturally to a baby after about the sixth month. Letting go of it again – as in a simple drop – is harder to learn, and intentionally throwing it is a future skill. This game lets your baby practice these first two skills while sharpening his eye-hand coordination.*

✔	**Eye-Hand Coordination**
✔	**Fine Motor Skills**
✔	**Grasp & Release**

IF YOUR BABY ENJOYS THIS ACTIVITY, also try Uh-Oh!, page 133.

135

TUNNEL TIME

PLACES TO GO

SKILLSPOTLIGHT

Crawling through *small spaces helps your baby learn just how big her body is in relation to other objects, which helps her develop both spatial and body awareness. This game also helps develop visual skills such as depth perception and builds her self-confidence as she maneuvers through the tunnel without the benefit of peripheral vision.*

Body Awareness	✔
Gross Motor Skills	✔
Spatial Awareness	✔

If your baby enjoys this activity, also try Obstacle Course, page 121.

EVER WONDER WHY your baby is so intent on wriggling under the bed, squeezing behind the couch, or curling up on the floor of your closet? A child this age is naturally intrigued with space — especially when it's just her size. You can cater to this fascination by providing a commercially made or cardboard tunnel for her to crawl through. Roll a ball down the tunnel and encourage her to go after it. Or put yourself, or small toys such as beanbags or plush toys, at the other end and coax her through.

SHE'S BOTH LEARNING ABOUT the nature of small spaces and enjoying the thrill of discovery when she crawls through a baby-sized tunnel.

RESEARCH REPORT

Educators have long believed *that children exhibit distinct learning styles, or preferences, for taking in new information. Some kids need to physically explore something in order to understand it, while others need simply to see or hear it. Today some researchers believe that even infants show such preferences, as evidenced by their tendency to look at, listen to, or fiddle with objects very intently. Since babies need to develop all their senses, it's a good idea for parents to continue to offer their babies stimulating new environments to explore.*

137

SING ABOUT ME

YOUR LITTLE ONE may not be able to say "mouth," "nose," "feet," or "toes," but he's probably already beginning to associate your spoken words with his body parts. You can boost his growing language and motor skills by teaching him these body songs. Gently move his arms and legs and use your hands and fingers to indicate the parts of his body.

PAT-A-CAKE

Pat-a-cake, pat-a-cake, baker's man,
clap hands together

bake me a cake as fast as you can.
clap hands

Pat it and prick it,
tap finger on one palm

and mark it with a B,
trace an imaginary B on one palm

and put it in the oven for Baby and me.
pretend to slide a cake into an oven

NOSE, NOSE, JOLLY RED NOSE

Nose, nose, jolly red nose –
tap your own nose

and who gave thee that jolly red nose?
point to baby's nose

Nutmeg and ginger, cinnamon and cloves –
wrinkle up your nose and pretend to sniff your palm

that's what gave me this jolly red nose.
tap baby's nose

HERE ARE THE TOES

 to the *tune* of **"Take Me Out to the Ball Game"**

Here are the toes of my (baby's name),
tap on baby's toes

**here are the toes of my (gal/guy),
and here are his feet and
his tiny knees –**
tap on baby's feet and knees

I can't help it – I'll give them a squeeze.
gently squeeze above baby's knees

**And he's got two arms
just for hugging,**
pat on baby's arms

and hands that clap and wave.
clap baby's hands for him

**But it's his eyes, nose,
mouth, and chin**
tap baby's facial features

that really draw me in!
lean in and kiss baby's face

HEY MR. KNICKERBOCKER

**Hey Mr. Knickerbocker,
boppity-bop,**
*standing with baby, rock
from side to side*

**I sure like the way you
walkity walk.**
lean baby forward and back

**I like the way you
walkity walk
with your feet,
ch-ch-ch-ch-ch-
ch-ch-ch-ch.**
walk forward

EYES, NOSE, FINGERS, and toes – your baby delights in Mommy's songs about him.

PUSH ME, PULL YOU

WALKING PRACTICE

SKILL SPOTLIGHT

The support provided by a pushable object allows your baby to practice walking without holding on to furniture or your hands. By now, your baby has learned a little about how her body works – how she can work against gravity to keep herself upright as she moves forward. Walking and pushing helps her develop balance and gross motor skills.

Balance	✔
Gross Motor Skills	✔
Lower-Body Strength	✔

IF YOUR BABY is walking, or even starting to toddle, she appreciates the support provided by a large object (like a push toy, stroller, or small chair) that she can push across the floor. A laundry basket filled with her toys also makes a great walking aid. You might help her at first by pulling from the other side – but then watch out! She will soon want to do it all by herself.

A MOVEABLE OBJECT that is just your baby's size provides support but lets her feel like she's walking all by herself.

"Look at my big girl go!"

MONKEY SEE

IMITATING OTHERS

Just Like Me

 to the *tune* of **"London Bridge Is Falling Down"**

**Make your hands go
clap clap clap,
clap clap clap,
clap clap clap.
Make your hands go
clap clap clap,
just like me.**

**Make your head go
side to side,
side to side,
side to side.
Make your head go
side to side,
just like me.**

MITATING OLDER PEOPLE – whether siblings, parents, or next-door neighbors – is a prime source of learning for an older baby, and you can turn that imitation instinct into a game. Slap your knees, bang the floor or high-chair tray, put your hands over your eyes, open your mouth wide, or tip your head from side to side as you sing a song. She'll learn new words for her body and its movements, and also discover the joy of an interactive game.

CREATING NEW SOUNDS while directing arm and finger movements helps your child develop auditory memory and rhythm.

| **Body Awareness** | ✔ |
| **Language Development** | ✔ |

142

UPSTAIRS, DOWNSTAIRS

LEARNING STAIR SAFETY

ONCE YOUR BABY CAN CRAWL across the floor, he'll be eager to try crawling up the stairs, too. Going up is easy. It's getting down that's hard. Rather than banning him from the stairs, teach your baby how to descend safely by helping him turn around on his belly— feet first— and find the stairs with his feet. Guidance is important at first. Use consistent cue phrases such as "turn around" or "feet first" each time he approaches the stairs. And don't let him head for the stairs on his own.

LEARNING HOW to climb and descend stairs safely is a crucial skill for all budding toddlers as well as a fun activity.

SKILL SPOTLIGHT

Learning to reach his feet *into a space he cannot see and then find firm footing teaches your baby a lot about spatial relations and balance. Stair practice also helps your baby develop a better sense of height and depth, which makes him more cautious in his future climbing pursuits.*

✔	**Balance**
✔	**Gross Motor Skills**
✔	**Lower-Body Strength**
✔	**Spatial Awareness**

143

PLAYING WITH YOUR TODDLER

WHETHER THEIR expressions are marked by ear-to-ear grins or brow-furrowing intensity, toddlers at play are a wonder to behold. The concentration with which they examine — and whoops! occasionally disassemble — each new object, the enthusiasm they bring to each new endeavor, and the joy they radiate as they acquire each new skill

A STRING OF BUB-BLES is a magical delight — and a dazzling demonstration of cause and effect.

demonstrate that for these young explorers, play is serious business. It's a way of learning about their world, other people, and themselves, of testing and pushing the limits of their abilities, of conquering everything from the physics of sand castles to the basic rules of social interaction.

These early years are ripe with unparalleled opportunities for you as a parent to unlock your child's potential. A toddler's brain is a work in progress profoundly influenced by her environment, and what she is now exposed to — or not exposed to — will have a lifelong impact. This might be a daunting prospect except for a few comforting facts. First, children are born primed to learn. Second, parents instinctively strive to provide the stimulation children need. And, most important, since play is a vehicle of learning for children, engaging in this task should be fun for parent and child alike.

THE BENEFITS OF PLAY

Because play comes so naturally to children and seems like nothing more than simple pleasure, it is easy to overlook the many far-reaching benefits that

COORDINATION and rhythm go hand in hand once she's picked up the beat of a catchy tune.

engrossed in a variety of play activities teaches him how to concentrate and persevere.

Play also provides an invaluable window to your child's personality. By playing with him — or watching him play with others — you will soon learn how he reacts to obstacles, failures, and victories. You'll see his quirky sense of humor emerge and his social skills begin to develop over time. His manner of playing can reveal his emotions, aptitudes, and preferred learning styles — whether he's responding well

play contributes to your child's emotional, physical, and intellectual development. Through play, a toddler learns so many vital skills — how to communicate, count, and solve problems. He hones his gross motor skills by tossing balls or climbing up a slide, and polishes his fine motor skills by painting with brushes or drawing with crayons. His imagination soars as he pretends to converse on a toy telephone or dons a succession of silly hats in front of a mirror. His language skills improve as he listens to stories and strives to communicate his needs and preferences. Early play encounters with his peers, siblings, parents, and other adults teach him how to get along with others and to respect rules and boundaries. Becoming

A SIMPLE JINGLE is a rockin' adventure when Mom's along for the ride.

to verbal instructions or visual images, for example, or if he retains information best after hands-on experiences.

Play also affords a wonderful opportunity for bonding with your toddler. When she is in a quiet mood, cuddling and looking at picture books or building an elaborate block tower creates a feeling of peaceful togetherness. When she's feeling a bit rowdier, a game of hide-and-seek or a beanbag toss imparts the notion that parents can be fun as well as sources of care and compassion. When you help her acquire new skills and praise her efforts, you convincingly demonstrate how you are always there to lend support and spur her progress — and countless studies demonstrate that children learn

A FEW RUBBER BALLS can teach a toddler worlds about distance, size, and shape.

best in a loving, supportive environment. In so many ways, being your child's enthusiastic play partner creates a special closeness that will resonate throughout both of your lives.

ROLLING TO THE MUSIC lets toddlers (and moms) exercise their rambunctious sides.

DIFFERENT WAYS TO PLAY

This section is designed to help you make the most of the wonderful toddler years by providing a wealth of simple and diverse activities to enjoy with your child. You'll find rousing fingerplays to sing along to, art projects, bath-time activities, games with blankets and boxes and blocks, as well as many other imaginative suggestions. There are ways to introduce children to the joys of music, to encourage muscular coordination and strength, and to build budding vocabularies. The wide variety of activities touches upon every important component of a child's physical, mental, social, and emotional skills, and each has been carefully designed and selected for developmental appropriateness. Some are classics, some are Gymboree's own innovations, but all are designed to foster the type of loving, nurturing interaction that helps a toddler learn and forms a lasting bond between parent and child.

Although playing and learning are inextricably linked, the point of these activities is not to run your toddler through a rigid battery of exercises. Instead, this section's emphasis is on having fun first and foremost through activities that also happen to spur age-appropriate development in your child. These activities help build a solid foundation for all future learning. In other words, they help your toddler learn *how* to learn.

READY, SET, PLAY!

Far from being rigid, the instructions in this book are intended as guidelines for loosely structured play, open to modification as you respond to your own child's particular interests and inclinations. Get things going, then step back and allow your toddler the freedom to explore

and experiment as he wishes. This is key to encouraging him to work things out on his own, learn to problem-solve, think creatively, and achieve self-esteem and a sense of autonomy.

Setting up a well-designed, safe play environment also contributes to his growing sense of independence and provides stimulation: deck the walls in his room with shatterproof mirrors and colorful

BRING ON THE NONSENSE — no song is too silly as far as your giggly wiggle-worm is concerned.

posters, and transform the ceiling into a starry sky or an undersea fantasy with glow-in-the-dark stickers. Arrange low bookcases or tables with a rotating assortment of toddler-friendly toys, books, and art supplies, providing bins for easy sorting and storage. Place a hamper within your child's reach, as well as a rack for hanging up clothes. Most important, don't think you need to stock up on a lot of expensive and elaborate playthings; classics such as puzzles, bubbles, puppets, blocks, tops, and balls remain versatile and engaging toddler toys.

As you become familiar with this book, feel free to return again and again to your child's favorite activities. Children benefit greatly from repetition. It allows them to test and refine what they have learned and it gives them a sense of accomplishment (for more on repetition, see page 176). And don't fret if your child doesn't seem to conform to the age bands listed — if your one-year-old, for instance, is having trouble handling the beach ball in Pass the Ball or, conversely, if your two-year-old quickly memorizes every song and fingerplay in the book. Keep in mind that each child develops at her own pace and in her own style (for more information on developmental differences, see page 160). The age bands are simply broad guidelines, and there are plenty of activities in this book to suit every child's unique needs and preferences.

So go ahead, put on your play clothes, warm up those vocal cords, and prepare to enter and enhance your toddler's world by trying the activities suggested in the following pages. They'll help you provide a richer, more stimulating environment for your child — and a treasury of happy memories for you, your child's first playmate.

FINGERPLAYS
help your itsy-bitsy spider flex her verbal as well as motor skills.

The following activities are grouped chronologically in six-month age ranges that match key stages in a child's development. These are general guidelines only, as there is a wide range of developmental differences among children.

12 MONTHS AND UP

Whether they're crawling, cruising, or walking, one-year-olds enjoy a newfound mobility that accompanies their enormous curiosity about the world. Their fine motor skills have developed to the point where they can assuredly pick up small objects and stack a few blocks. They love listening to their parents' voices, such as when reading a story or singing a song. They understand many words and respond to some simple commands; most also begin saying a few words of their own.

18 MONTHS AND UP

Children this age are determined to explore, handle, taste, and shake, rattle, and roll everything in sight. Their increasingly sophisticated gross motor skills allow them to walk, run, and climb, and their fine motor skills permit them to eat with a spoon and throw a ball. They enjoy games that engage their tactile senses and can express an appreciation of music by swaying. Their vocabulary averages more than a dozen words, and they can usually form simple two- and three-word phrases.

24 MONTHS AND UP

Children's strength, flexibility, and balance are stronger and surer now: they can unscrew the lid of a jar and perform other tasks that showcase their developing fine motor abilities. Their enthusiasm for music continues, and they are beginning to use their imaginations. Most enjoy the company of peers, although rather than engaging in joint activities they tend to play independently side by side. Two-year-olds might have more than two hundred words in their vocabulary, and they begin to speak in simple sentences.

30 MONTHS AND UP

Older toddlers delight in activities that refine and stretch their physical abilities, such as running, jumping, tricycle riding, and playing a simple game of catch. They continue to hone their fine motor skills, such as holding a crayon or paintbrush. Their attention spans increase, and they often show a passion for classifying activities and sorting games. Their fluency with language grows dramatically, and they catch on to the notion of abstractions, making for a rich repertoire of fantasy play.

151

PASS THE BALL

BALL PLAY FOR BEGINNERS

SKILLSPOTLIGHT

Learning to roll *or even stop a ball helps toddlers refine their gross motor skills and develop eye-hand (or eye-foot, as the case may be) coordination. Playing with balls helps them develop a sense of timing as they attempt to figure out how long it will take before the ball reaches them.*

Body Awareness	✔
Coordination	✔
Gross Motor Skills	✔

IF YOUR CHILD ENJOYS THIS ACTIVITY, also try Tube Tricks, page 218. ▶

FEW TODDLERS can actually catch a ball – that takes a good bit of coordination – but most love to push, kick, and grab this engaging toy. To start your toddler out on ball play, choose a flat, grassy spot outside or a cleared space inside, and sit just a couple of feet away from her. Gently roll the ball to your child and encourage her to roll it back in your direction. As she gets better at it, sit farther and farther away. Try softly bouncing the ball between the two of you, as well.

A BALL THAT'S ABOUT THE SIZE of your child's head is just right; it's not so big that it will overwhelm her and not so small that she'll have trouble handling it.

12 MONTHS AND UP
1

THE FINGER BAND

A SONG WITH IMAGINARY INSTRUMENTS

IT'S NEVER TOO EARLY to give your toddler music lessons, especially when the instruments are make-believe. As you sing "The Finger Band" (lyrics at right), pretend to play different instruments such as drums, a flute, cymbals, and a piano. Don't worry if your child has never heard a clarinet, much less seen a trombone — she will enjoy watching and imitating your hand movements. Make your gestures distinct and energetic. If at first she can't copy you, move her hands and fingers for her. As she gets more coordinated, march your legs up and down as you sing and play. Alternate between singing softly and loudly, explaining the difference as you do so.

PROP YOUR LITTLE MAJORETTE on your lap and introduce her to your finger band before launching into this musical parade.

 to the *tune* of **"The Mulberry Bush"**

**The finger band has come to town,
come to town, come to town,
the finger band has come to town,
so early in the morning.**
hold up and wiggle your fingers

**The finger band can play the drums,
play the drums, play the drums,
the finger band can play the drums,
so early in the morning.**
pantomime playing a drum

**The finger band can play the flute,
play the flute, play the flute,
the finger band can play the flute,
so early in the morning.**
pantomime playing a flute and continue with other instruments

✓	**Eye-Hand Coordination**
✓	**Language Development**
✓	**Listening Skills**

153

PARACHUTE PLAY

FUN WAYS TO BUILD BALANCING SKILLS

SKILLSPOTLIGHT

Parachute play *enhances your toddler's ability to balance – a skill that translates to freedom and independence, because it's a precursor to walking, running, and more complex physical actions such as skipping or even doing a somersault. Parachutes are also intrinsically interesting items to use because of their slick feel and bold colors; reinforce your child's color-recognition skills by naming the colors as you play.*

Balance	✔
Tactile Stimulation	✔
Visual Discrimination	✔

YOUR TODDLER will cheer as you treat him to a slip-and-slide parachute ride, and in the process you'll safely challenge his ability to balance while in motion. On a carpeted floor, seat or lay him on a colorful mini-parachute, blanket, or sheet, then gently and gradually pull him around, taking care to avoid any furniture and sharp corners as you explore the great indoors.

• Recruit another adult to help you hold the blanket or parachute over your child's head. If your child can stand with ease, test his balance by slowly raising and lowering the parachute while he stands underneath it and admires the colors or pattern. Do this carefully; even a lightweight parachute can topple an unsteady toddler.

WHO NEEDS A MAGIC CARPET? Being transported by Daddy on a colorful parachute, sheet, or blanket is a toddler's dream come true.

• Walking in a circle, hold the blanket or parachute over your toddler's head singing "Ring Around the Rosy" (see Circle Songs, page 234, for the lyrics) or another appropriate song that your child likes. At the end of the song, let the parachute float down to the floor over your toddler. The more the merrier when a group of kids joins in the fun.

IF YOUR CHILD ENJOYS THIS ACTIVITY, also try Freeze Dance, page 165.

BUBBLE BUSTERS

A POP-THE-BUBBLE GAME OF CHASE

SKILLSPOTLIGHT

Chasing, catching, *and popping bubbles contributes to eye-hand coordination, sensory stimulation, body awareness, and gross motor skills. And if your toddler tries to blow bubbles herself, she'll learn about cause and effect. Your bubble buster is also discovering that when she touches an apparently solid object, it sometimes pops – her first lesson in physics!*

MAKING YOUR OWN

For the soap solution, mix 1 cup of water, 1 tablespoon of glycerin (available in most pharmacies), and 2 tablespoons of dishwashing detergent. Fashion bubble wands from pipe cleaners, plastic bag ties, even plastic cups with the bottom cut out.

Eye-Hand Coordination	✔
Gross Motor Skills	✔
Language Development	✔
Tactile Stimulation	✔

IF THERE IS A MAGIC EQUATION for entrancing a toddler, it must be the combination of a simple soap solution and a bubble wand. Blowing, chasing, and popping bubbles is an excellent opportunity to encourage movement, stimulate eye-hand coordination, and introduce the concepts of big and small, high and low. Experiment with an assortment of bubble wands in varying sizes. Don't be surprised if your toddler enjoys this activity so much that "bubble" becomes one of her favorite words!

• Use a large wand to make big bubbles and cheer her as she chases and pops them, then repeat the activity with a smaller wand. Blow forcefully when you're creating a shower of tiny bubbles and softly when you're making a huge bubble. Blow the bubbles up high and down low, saying "high" or "low" as they float away.

• When you blow bubbles outdoors, explain that the wind that rustles the leaves and blows her hair also carries the bubbles away. Encourage your toddler to pop the bubbles with her fingers or stomp on them with her feet. Walk backward as you blow on the bubble wand so she'll chase you to catch the bubbles.

A BIG SHOWER OF BUBBLES will fascinate your little one. And when she chases and pops them, she'll be exercising her eye-hand coordination and gross motor skills.

CLAP, CLAP, CLAP

A MOVE-YOUR-BODY SONG

SKILL SPOTLIGHT

Learning the words for body parts, and learning to control those hands, arms, and feet, is serious business for kids this age. While your toddler may already be pointing to her body parts when you name them, this song gives her a chance to practice isolating and moving her hands, feet, arms, and lips.

Body Awareness	✔
Gross Motor Skills	✔
Listening Skills	✔
Social Skills	✔

IF YOUR CHILD ENJOYS THIS ACTIVITY, also try Just Like Me, page 181. ▶

IF YOU'RE FAMILIAR with the ever-popular song "The Wheels on the Bus" (see page 168), you can add a new twist to the tune with these lyrics (right). "Clap, Clap, Clap" coaxes your little one to coordinate body movements with words. Associating words and actions with a melody and a beat will enhance her understanding of rhythm, because she'll be able to feel it and mimic it with her body.

• Young toddlers are eager to learn the words for body parts, so be sure to emphasize those words in the song – "hands," "arms," "mouth" – by enunciating them or singing them more loudly. Make big motions at first to underscore the meaning of the words.

• Try variations: ask your child to tap her knees, shake her hips, or nod her head.

• After she's learned the song, make a few "mistakes" – clap your hands when you're supposed to be tapping your foot. Her laughter shows she already has a sense of humor.

YOUR TODDLER WILL ENJOY imitating you as you clap your hands and tap your foot in this music game.

158

12 MONTHS
1
AND UP

 to the tune of **"The Wheels on the Bus"**

**You take your little hands
and go clap, clap, clap,**
clap your hands
**clap, clap, clap,
clap, clap, clap.
You take your little hands
and go clap, clap, clap,
clap your little hands.**

**You take your little foot
and go tap, tap, tap,**
tap your foot
**tap, tap, tap,
tap, tap, tap.
You take your little foot
and go tap, tap, tap,
tap your little foot.**

**You take your little arms
and go hug, hug, hug,**
hug each other
**hug, hug, hug,
hug, hug, hug.**

**You take your little arms
and go hug, hug, hug,
hug your mom and dad.**

**You take your little mouth
and go kiss, kiss, kiss,**
pucker your lips
**kiss, kiss, kiss,
kiss, kiss, kiss.
You take your little mouth
and go kiss, kiss, kiss,
kiss your mom and dad.**

**You take your little hand
and wave bye, bye, bye,**
wave good-bye
**bye, bye, bye,
bye, bye, bye.
You take your little hand
and wave bye, bye, bye,
wave your little hand.**

159

AT THEIR OWN PACE

BABIES SIT UP at six months. They utter their first "dada" at nine. They crawl at seven months and walk at age one. When parents are confronted by the firm developmental timetables sometimes espoused in popular child-care books, they often are pleased if their children achieve a milestone a few weeks or months ahead of schedule – and panicked if their offspring are late. But while pediatricians used to treat these timetables as if they were carved in granite, most practitioners today agree that there is a much wider developmental range in perfectly healthy children.

A child may first roll over, for example, at any time from two to six months of age. Children can vary the age at which they start talking by a year or more, and future soccer stars may take their first steps as early as seven months and as late as eighteen. Although children generally follow the prescribed developmental sequence, some will skip a milestone completely – they might never learn to crawl, for example. Instead, when their muscle tone and coordination skills are ready, they just get up and start walking.

All of these developmental milestones are a matter of complex neural and muscular maturation, which is affected by both inherited and environmental factors – a child may walk late in life, for example, if the family has a history of late walkers. Often a child lags in one area while accelerating in another. In rare instances, a delayed milestone can signal significant problems, but in the vast majority of cases it's just a matter of a child developing at her own rate. As educational psychologist Jane Healy observes in her book *Your Child's Growing Mind:* "A child who is lagging slightly in development is on the same track as the others. His train simply goes at a slower pace, although it stands every chance of reaching the same destination." ▪

ITSY-BITSY SPIDER

12 MONTHS
1
AND UP

A FAVORITE FIRST FINGERPLAY

IN THIS POPULAR SONG, you can portray the trials of the hapless itsy-bitsy spider with fun-to-mimic hand motions. By repeating the song and the gestures you are not only entertaining your toddler, you're also stimulating her listening and language skills. Add tactile stimulation by crawling the spider up her tummy, "pouring" the rain down over her shoulders, and crossing her arms above her head to make the sun. When she seems proficient, try singing the song and cuing her to perform the finger movements – eventually she may surprise you with a solo rendition.

**The itsy-bitsy spider
went up the water spout,**
walk your fingers up in the air

**down came the rain and
washed the spider out.**
*wiggle your fingers downward
to make rain*

**Out came the sun and
dried up all the rain,**
*form a circle with your
fingers above your head*

**and the itsy-bitsy spider
went up the spout again.**
walk your fingers up again

✔	**Fine Motor Skills**
✔	**Listening Skills**
✔	**Tactile Stimulation**

MIMING THE TRAVAILS of the itsy-bitsy spider with you not only promotes your toddler's listening and language abilities, it helps her develop fine motor skills.

161

THE PILLOW COURSE

FIRST STEPS ON A PATH OF PILLOWS

SKILLSPOTLIGHT

Movement and exploration *are near and dear to a toddler's heart, so an opportunity to move around in an interesting environment is bound to be met with joy. This activity is also an excellent way for your toddler to build his motor skills by challenging large muscle groups and to increase both his balance and coordination as he faces physical obstacles.*

Balance	✔
Body Awareness	✔
Eye-Foot Coordination	✔
Gross Motor Skills	✔

CREATE A SAFE OBSTACLE COURSE in your living room by laying out a simple zigzagging path of pillows and cushions.

• Encourage your child to complete the course by crawling or walking along the path. It will be a bumpy, lumpy route, so even if he's already walking be sure to hold on to his hands as he begins the journey. Once he becomes more sure-footed, let him take some steps on the pillows by himself, but stay nearby just in case he starts to topple. Remove your toddler's shoes and socks to help him keep his balance.

• Vary the height of the path by stacking a couple of pillows. To make the course more challenging, run it under a table so he has to crawl underneath, or position pillows around the room so he must maneuver around soft furniture (avoid furniture with sharp edges).

• Use cushions and pillows of varying sizes, colors, and textures to keep the course interesting. Don't be surprised if your young athlete stops occasionally to feel the obstacles with his hands or feet. Allow him to explore, then gently encourage him to keep going.

IF YOUR CHILD ENJOYS THIS ACTIVITY, also try Parachute Play, page 154.

RESEARCH REPORT

The wide range in age *at which children begin walking – anytime from seven to eighteen months – reflects the complexity of this deceptively simple act. The mind as well as the body is involved in venturing those first steps, and it takes time for nerve cells to operate smoothly, allowing deliberate and controlled movement. A child also must build up sufficient muscle tone in his legs and hone his sense of balance and coordination, skills toddlers acquire at different rates.*

HE'S ON THE WAY to walking when he follows a trail of cushions around the house – with Daddy's help, of course.

12 MONTHS
1
AND UP

HATS ON!

EXPERIMENTING WITH DIFFERENT HEADGEAR

SKILLSPOTLIGHT

Talking to your toddler *about the hats the two of you are wearing helps expose him to new words that will someday become a part of his vocabulary. And seeing you in different hats teaches him that you're still Mommy even if you look a little different. When your child is a bit older, he'll start to enjoy role-playing with the hats, a game that will stretch his capacity for imaginative play.*

Concept Development	✔
Language Development	✔
Social Skills	✔

YOUR **YOUNG ONE GRINS** when you put your baseball cap on backward. Now watch his face light up as you put a parade of special hats on his head, too. Pick up fun gear at thrift stores or perhaps in Grandma's attic. Then try it on and giggle together in front of a mirror. This is a good opportunity to help expand your child's vocabulary by using adjectives to describe the hats ("This hat is red" or "The feathers are soft").

• As your toddler gets closer to age two, he'll be able to revel in role-playing as he tries on different hats.

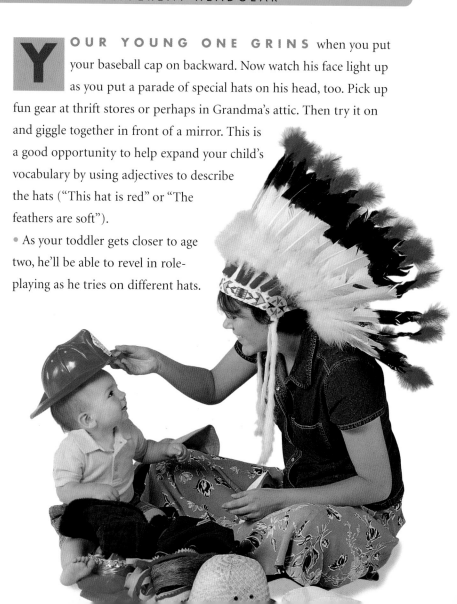

Y̲OUR TODDLER WILL MARVEL at your elaborate headdress and smile when you make him a fire chief — especially if you mimic special sound effects, such as an engine siren, to go with each hat.

12 MONTHS
1
AND UP

FREEZE DANCE

STOP-AND-GO MUSICAL FUN

PLAY MUSIC and put a friend or older child in charge of the volume control while you take your young dancer for a twirl. Hold your toddler in your arms; when the music starts, exaggerate your dance moves by swaying from side to side and dipping her on occasion. When the music stops, hold your stance; begin dancing when the music starts again, then freeze each time it halts. Older toddlers may be able to dance – and stop – on their own, but most are just as happy to "freeze" in your embrace.

SKILLSPOTLIGHT

By taking a ride *in your arms as you dance the night away, your toddler experiences the rhythm of music, a crucial first step in developing both language and music skills. And when you freeze in mid-action, she learns to balance herself in your arms. Suddenly turning the music on and off gives your toddler something she dearly loves – a surprise – and cultivates listening skills as well.*

✔	**Balance**
✔	**Listening Skills**
✔	**Social Skills**

SWINGING TO THE BEAT is a surefire way to thrill her – especially when you surprise her with sudden pauses in your boogie.

165

TWINKLE, TWINKLE

SOME SONGS ENDURE generation after generation, giving parents and grandparents a chance to share their old favorites with young children. But old favorites can be changed in new and surprising ways, so as you sing these suggested variations of "Twinkle, Twinkle Little Star," try to come up with some simple – or silly – improvisations of your own.

SHE'LL BE ENCHANTED when you sing and mime the old standby "Twinkle, Twinkle Little Star"– but there are countless variations if you want to try new lyrics.

TWINKLE, TWINKLE LITTLE STAR

Twinkle, twinkle little star,
hold hands up, opening and closing fists
how I wonder what you are!

Up above the world so high,
point upward
like a diamond in the sky.
create a diamond with thumbs and forefingers

Twinkle, twinkle little star,
open and close fists
how I wonder what you are!

THE APPLE TREE

 to the ***tune*** *of* **"Twinkle, Twinkle Little Star"**

Way up high in the apple tree
stretch arms up high
two little apples
looking down at me.
make circles around eyes with thumbs
and forefingers

I shook that tree
just as hard as I could,
shake an imaginary tree with
both hands
down came the apples
float fingers down
and mmm they were good!
rub tummy and smile

I shook that tree
just as hard as I could,
shake an imaginary tree with
both hands
down came the apples
float fingers down
and mmm they were good!
rub tummy and smile

THE SKY SO BLUE

 to the ***tune*** *of* **"Twinkle, Twinkle Little Star"**

Way up in the sky so blue
reach up to the sky with both hands
two little clouds said "peekaboo."
play peekaboo with hands

The wind blew the clouds
just as hard as it could,
rub hands together and shiver
down came the raindrops
flutter fingers down
and oooh. . . they felt good!

The wind blew the clouds
just as hard as it could,
rub hands together
and shiver
down came the raindrops
flutter fingers down
and oooh. . . they felt good!

167

THE WHEELS ON THE BUS

A MUSICAL TRANSPORTATION TOUR

SKILLSPOTLIGHT

The catchy tune and easy-to-follow gestures make this sing-along a skill-building activity for all toddlers. Repeating the song stimulates your toddler's auditory development, while the hand movements help him conceptualize what the words mean. As his motor skills and memory improve, he will readily imitate most of the hand gestures and even begin to anticipate many of them.

Body Awareness	✔
Concept Development	✔
Coordination	✔
Language Development	✔
Listening Skills	✔

THIS SONG is an all-time toddler classic. You can perform it in many ways, but it's easiest with your child seated facing you or on your lap facing away from you. If he's propped up on your lap, gently guide his hands through the movements.

• Begin by showing him the different motions as you sing, then encourage him to join in.

• Don't be afraid to improvise your own verses and corresponding hand movements if the spirit moves you – your toddler will love it!

TAKE A FAVORITE PASSENGER for a ride on the bus, showing him how the wheels go round and round and the wipers go swish, swish, swish.

168

The wheels on the bus go round and round,
roll forearms forward in a circular motion

round and round,
continue to roll arms

round and round.
roll arms

The wheels on the bus go round and round,
roll arms

all through the town.
draw a circle in the air

The horn on the bus goes beep, beep, beep,
press imaginary horn with hand

beep, beep, beep,
press horn with hand

beep, beep, beep.
press horn with hand

The horn on the bus goes beep, beep, beep,
press horn with hand

all through the town.
draw a circle in the air

continue with:
The wipers on the bus go swish, swish, swish . . .
sway forearms back and forth

The driver on the bus says "Move on back" . . .
point over your shoulder with your thumb

The lights on the bus go blink, blink, blink . . .
open and close fists

The baby on the bus goes waah, waah, waah . . .
make cradling motion with your arms

The parents on the bus say "I love you" . . .
hug your child

IF YOUR CHILD ENJOYS THIS ACTIVITY, also try Itsy-Bitsy Spider, page 161.

BAND ON THE RUN

MUSIC FROM THE KITCHEN CABINET

SKILL SPOTLIGHT

One way toddlers learn *cause and effect is by making sounds with a variety of objects. As a child bangs on a bowl, he learns that he is capable of creating sounds by himself. As he practices, he improves his coordination and his understanding of rhythm, and as he experiments with the various "instruments" in his cabinet, he learns that he can create a myriad of interesting (and loud!) sounds.*

CLEAR OUT A KITCHEN CUPBOARD (near the floor) for your child and fill it with sturdy wooden spoons, metal bowls of different sizes, lightweight pans (cake pans and small frying pans work well), wooden salad bowls, metal lids of various sizes, and plastic measuring cups. The greater the variety of "instruments," the greater the variety of sounds you and your toddler will be able to make, so be creative as you stock the cupboard. If you have toy instruments on hand, add them to the mix.

• With older toddlers, create a stop-and-go band. Have your child bang on the "instruments" while listening to you – the bandleader – give directions to stop the music and start it again.

• As your young musician plays, encourage him to experiment with sound by banging in different ways: with enthusiasm, gently, slowly, fast. Demonstrate to show him the difference.

• Play music (tunes with a strong beat are best) and encourage him to add his own percussion sounds.

Cause & Effect	✔
Coordination	✔
Listening Skills	✔
Rhythm Exploration	✔

EVERYTHING BUT THE KITCHEN SINK – and that would probably work as well – is a potential instrument for a budding musician.

The raucous noise that results from your toddler's kitchen concert is actually good "brain food," says educational psychologist Jane Healy. "Toys with sound or visual input improve cognitive skills, but it is important that [your child] be able to interact with them. Banging two pans together is far better . . . than pushing buttons to create noises produced by hidden electronic parts. The child should be able to link cause and effect – and see the parts of the toy at work."

171

PEEKABOO BOXES

PUTTING NAMES TO FAMILIAR FACES

SKILL SPOTLIGHT

This activity refines *your child's visual memory and fine motor skills. Most significantly, matching a word with its visual representation helps build the language skills he'll need later, when he begins reading and writing. As your child's vocabulary expands, surprise him now and then by pasting new pictures inside the boxes.*

COLLECT AN ASSORTMENT of cigar boxes, shoe boxes, or gift boxes. Cut out pictures of family members or easily recognizable objects (such as household items, animals, or toys) and paste one inside the lid of each box. Open the boxes and discuss the images inside. As your child's confidence grows, ask him to open the boxes and name the pictures. Once he masters this (around two years of age), test his memory: ask him which box contains the picture of Daddy, a horse, or a ball.

FINDING A PHOTO of Mommy, Daddy, or the family dog under the lid of a box is a great way to boost your little one's sense of discovery while enhancing his visual memory.

Fine Motor Skills	✔
Language Development	✔
Social Skills	✔
Visual Memory	✔

172

FUNNY FEET

EXPLORING TEXTURE WITH YOUR TOES

EVEN A CHILD who has been toddling for several months is still getting used to the sensations involved in walking. Take advantage of her curiosity by removing her shoes and leading her outside across a variety of textures, such as warm sand, smooth pebbles, cool concrete, wet grass, and gooey mud. As she gets older, ask her what she feels as she's walking. If she doesn't know the words yet, suggest some: "warm," "prickly," "soft." If you're worried about dirty feet, finish off by stomping in a basin of warm, soapy water.

YOUR TODDLER WILL DELIGHT in the feel of different textures, such as soft grass, on her sensitive soles. Kick off your shoes and join in the fun!

SKILL SPOTLIGHT

Walking barefoot *is easier for your young toddler than walking with shoes because she can use her toes to help with balance. And while the sensations of walking on unusual surfaces may make her giggle, she'll start to grasp the properties associated with different materials, as well as a few words to describe them.*

✔ **Body Awareness**

✔ **Language Development**

✔ **Sensory Exploration**

✔ **Tactile Discrimination**

173

PICTURE THIS

GROWING A BOOKWORM

SKILLSPOTLIGHT

Reading is an important tool *for learning language. Toddlers learn most of the rules of grammar simply by hearing you and others speak. And recent studies show that the size of a toddler's vocabulary depends on how much speech she hears in a meaningful context. So the more you read to your child, the easier it will be for her to develop strong language skills.*

Language Development	✔
Listening Skills	✔
Visual Discrimination	✔
Visual Memory	✔

SHE MAY NOT BE ABLE to talk and she may not understand all your words, but even a young toddler loves to "read books" with a parent or grandparent. The rhythm of the words engages her; the pictures teach her about her world.

• Choose books with clear pictures of familiar objects and point them out to your child as you read. It will help her learn the words for everyday things, such as "chair," "house," and "car."

• Select books made of cloth, plastic, or heavy cardboard. They can withstand toddlers' eager jaws and paws more readily than paper. And small books with padded covers are easier for little hands to handle.

• Edit out long narratives and hard words. Instead, abridge the plot and spend time talking about the illustrations or photographs. That will keep her interested and help her develop observational skills.

• Emphasize the rhymes and funny words that engage her.

• Tailor your reading session to her attention span. Let her wander off to play with her toys when she wants to. Ending the session while it's still fun will ensure that you're building a positive association with reading that will last a lifetime.

EVEN A CHILD who is too young to understand the plot will delight in the colorful pictures, the simple rhymes, and the cadence of Grandma's voice.

Although teachers *often exhort parents to read to their school-age children, a report by the Carnegie Corporation found that only half of all American babies and toddlers receive this attention. Yet early exposure to these important tools of learning and pleasure, as Penelope Leach writes in* Your Baby and Child, *helps children "to make friends with [books] and learn to value them." She recommends that parents introduce their toddler to a variety of both picture and story books, and suggests they spend a lot of time talking about the illustrations. "'Reading' pictures," Leach explains, "is a necessary start toward reading text."*

REPETITION IN PLAY

THINK YOU'LL GO nuts if you have to spend another minute rolling a ball back and forth with your toddler? Bored with reading his favorite book over and over again? Or maybe you're just worried that your child needs more variety in his play and you feel you should try to keep him from returning again and again to a few preferred activities.

Although it may try your patience, never underestimate the value of repetition when it comes to a child's development. As educational psychologist Jane Healy says in her book *Your Child's Growing Mind,* "An activity must be repeated many times to firm up neural networks for proficiency." In other words, by repeating the same story to your child every evening you are helping to stimulate the brain cells that allow your child to make the association between words and the objects they represent. And when it comes to rolling that ball, you'll soon see how his eye-hand coordination improves. A simple activity such as this helps prime him for more complex tasks in coming years, whether it's understanding the nuances in James Joyce's *Ulysses* or playing little-league baseball.

Besides, kids don't get bored as easily as adults do. As neurologist Ann Barnet notes in *The Youngest Minds,* "Nursery rhymes and simple games enthrall small children precisely because they become familiar." Mastering a new skill gives them a lot of confidence and even whets their appetites for future challenges.

This isn't to say that parents can't overdo it by spending too much time interacting on one activity with their child — even young minds and bodies can get overtaxed. So be sure to take your cues from your child: watch for signs of frustration or restlessness, but if he's enjoying an activity, let him do it . . . over and over and over again. ■

FUN-FILLED JARS

FINDING OUT WHAT'S INSIDE

COLLECT A FEW LARGE, clear plastic jars with easy-to-remove lids. Place a favorite toy or colorful scarf inside each jar and close the lid. Ask your child to take off the lid and pull out the toy or scarf. (You might need to start this activity with loose lids so her not-so-nimble fingers can remove the toys more easily.) Your toddler will be eager to remove the toys again and again. When you're filling the jars, select toys that are more than 1¾ inches (4.5 cm) in diameter (so there won't be a choking hazard).

A TOY INSIDE a jar provides plenty of incentive to lift off the lid.

SKILLSPOTLIGHT

Learning to remove a lid, *even if it's already unscrewed, helps your toddler develop coordination and fine motor skills. And just attempting to unscrew a lid enhances these skills as well. In this activity, success is immediately rewarded, ensuring that your toddler will want to try removing the lids again and again.*

✔	**Fine Motor Skills**
✔	**Language Development**
✔	**Social Skills**

IF YOUR CHILD ENJOYS THIS ACTIVITY, also try Cereal Challenge, page 202.

177

SILLY LAP SONGS

SITTING ON A PARENT'S LAP is not a passive activity for a busy toddler. Although your lap is a safe haven for your child – a place to relax and cuddle between activities – it's also associated with such pleasures as reading, rocking, and singing the following songs – and pretending to be an airplane, a pony, or even a funny frog.

THE AIRPLANE SONG

 to the *tune* of "Row, Row, Row, Your Boat"

**Fly, fly, fly your plane,
fly your plane up high.
Merrily, merrily, merrily, merrily,
high up in the sky!**

*hold your child firmly with both
hands and raise him overhead*

MAKE YOUR TODDLER feel secure
as he soars like a plane by looking at him,
smiling, and having as much fun as he is.

178

DOWN BY THE BANKS

Down by the banks of the hanky panky,
where the bullfrogs jump
from bank to banky.
They went oops, opps, belly flops.
One missed the lily pad
and went . . . kerplop!

*bounce your child on your lap as you teach
her this song; holding her securely, let her slip
partway between your legs on "kerplop"*

TROT LITTLE PONY

 to the tune of **"Hush Little Baby"**

Trot little pony, trot to town,
trot little pony, don't slow down.
Don't spill the buttermilk,
don't spill the eggs,
trot little pony, trot to town.

*holding your toddler securely on
your lap, gently bounce her up
and down*

WHEN WE ALL ROLL OVER

 to the tune of **"Have You Ever Seen a Lassie"**

When we all roll over,
roll over, roll over,
when we all roll over,
how happy we'll be!

Roll this way, and that way,
and this way, and that way,
when we all roll over,
how happy we'll be!

*bounce your toddler on your
lap as you sing, or, lying on
your back, place him facedown
on your stomach and rock him
gently from side to side*

179

I HAVE A LITTLE DUCK

MAKING WAVES WITH A SONG

 to the *tune* of **"The Wheels on the Bus"**

**I have a little duck that says
quack, quack, quack,
quack, quack, quack,
quack, quack, quack,
I have a little duck that says
quack, quack, quack,
all day long.**
"quack" your hands to the beat

**I have a little duck that goes
splash, splash, splash . . .**
splash the water gently

**I have a little duck that goes
swim, swim, swim . . .**
skim your hands on the surface

Cause & Effect	✔
Language Development	✔
Listening Skills	✔
Rhythm Exploration	✔
Sensory Exploration	✔

SHARE THIS FAMILIAR TUNE with your child as you play in the baby pool or bathtub – and use a family of rubber ducks as colorful props. Your toddler won't need much encouragement to splash, so be sure you are both ready to get wet. In the first verse, "quack" your hands (place your palms together as if you're miming a duck bill) in the water. Little will your toddler know that in the midst of all the hilarity, you are stimulating her auditory memory and enhancing her sense of rhythm.

YOUR DARLING DUCKLING will have fun playing in the water while watching you quack and splash to the beat of this cheery song.

JUST LIKE ME

A FOLLOW-THE-LEADER SONG

MAKE THE MOST of your toddler's natural instinct to mimic with this lively activity. Give yourself plenty of room and either sit with your child on your lap or stand facing him. Emphasize the name of each body part as you sing and point it out on your toddler's body as you make the movements. If your child is hesitant, gently help him raise and lower his arms, shoulders, and legs. Between repetitions of the song, ask him to point to his own arms or legs. Once he's following you like a pro, try adding some movements of your own invention.

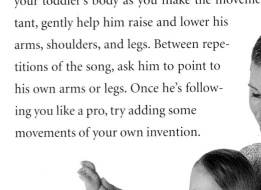

SHOWING YOUR TODDLER how to make his arms go up while singing this song is a fun way to introduce him to the names of his body parts.

to the *tune* of **"London Bridge Is Falling Down"**

**Make your arms go up and down,
up and down, up and down,
make your arms go up and down,
just like me.**

Continue with:
**Move your hands up and down . . .
Move your shoulders up and down . . .
Flap your elbows up and down . . .
Make your legs go up and down . . .
Move your feet up and down . . .
Move your body up and down . . .**

✔	**Body Awareness**
✔	**Concept Development**
✔	**Coordination**
✔	**Creative Movement**
✔	**Listening Skills**

181

A STAR IS BORN

TALKING ON TAPE

SKILLSPOTLIGHT

As you may have noticed, *your toddler is quite focused on herself at this stage – and with all things belonging to her. Just as a mirror intrigues her because she can see herself, a tape recording lets her revel in the sound of her voice. This helps her develop her listening skills, which are crucial to language development.*

Language Development	✔
Listening Skills	✔
Social Skills	✔

YOU'VE SEEN HOW your little one perks up at the sound of other children's voices. And you've noticed how she responds to seeing her face in the mirror. Now imagine her delight upon hearing a "reflection" of her own voice! Recording your child's voice gives her a whole new sense of herself and gives your entire family an audio baby journal to cherish for years to come.

• Record your toddler's sounds – laughing at Daddy's funny faces, babbling to herself as she plays, talking on a toy phone (see Ring-a-Ling, page 237), or shrieking with glee in the tub.

• Try recording a session the next time you read to your toddler. Later, she can listen to your story-time voice and her own commentary.

• You can use a cassette recorder with a built-in microphone, but a separate microphone that can be plugged into the recorder will provide a sharper sound.

• When your young crooner is older, around age two or three, encourage her to sing songs on tape – alone or with you or her friends.

IF YOUR CHILD ENJOYS THIS ACTIVITY, also try Mirror, Mirror, page 184. ▶

ONCE YOUR STARLET understands the purpose of the microphone, she'll reach for it and talk into it enthusiastically, which allows her to experience herself in a whole different way.

RESEARCHREPORT

Recent studies show *that the size of a toddler's vocabulary depends largely on how much her caregivers talk to her. University of Chicago researcher Janellen Huttenlocher found that 20-month-olds whose mothers had the gift of gab were shown to have about 130 more words in their vocabulary than same-age children with less talkative moms. By age two, the gap had doubled. But planting a child in front of a TV won't do: the interaction between child and speaker, and a connection to real-life events, is necessary for all of those precious words to soak in.*

MIRROR, MIRROR

GETTING TO KNOW ME

SKILLSPOTLIGHT

A sense of herself as a person *(hence her intrigue with the notions of I and mine versus you and yours) is key to your toddler's development. Playing with mirrors helps her develop this concept of self as separate from others. Toddlers are also intrigued with their bodies; labeling the parts of her body in front of the mirror helps her understand the names of those parts and encourages her to further explore her own identity.*

Body Awareness	✔
Language Development	✔
Self-Concept	✔
Social Skills	✔
Visual Discrimination	✔

YOUR CHILD has no doubt been fascinated with her own image since she was a wee baby. But mirror fun really begins in toddlerhood, because now she understands that the image is of herself — and understanding herself and all her body parts are her primary interests.

Sit or stand together in front of a mirror and make faces — happy, sad, and goofy. With an older toddler, encourage her to follow suit. Then point out her arms, legs, eyes, nose, and other body parts. Point out your own, as well.

Ask her who's the baby and who's the mommy — pretty soon she'll surprise you by pointing to the right image.

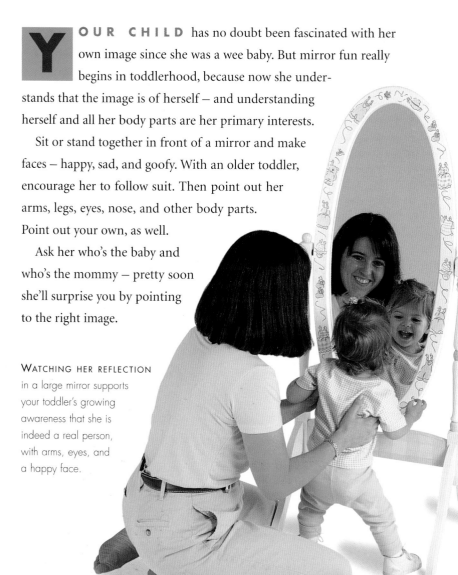

WATCHING HER REFLECTION in a large mirror supports your toddler's growing awareness that she is indeed a real person, with arms, eyes, and a happy face.

184

HEY MR. KNICKERBOCKER

PLAYING IN A ONE-KID BAND

SEAT YOUR TODDLER on your lap or on the floor in front of you for this favorite chant with silly sound effects. Create a slow beat by alternately slapping your hands on the floor and then clapping them together. Encourage your child to clap with you once you begin the chant. Repeat the chant's first two lines before you make a new motion and sound. When your toddler attempts to control his body to make a specific type of sound — such as stomping his feet or clicking his teeth — he improves both his language and motor skills.

ENTERTAIN EACH OTHER with all the funny sounds you make while repeating this favorite chant.

Hey Mr. Knickerbocker, boppity, bop!
pat your hands flat on the floor once, clap, then repeat

I like the way you boppity, bop!
continue alternately patting and clapping to establish a beat

Listen to the sound we make with our hands.
rub palms to make a chafing sound

Listen to the sound we make with our feet.
stomp feet loudly on floor to the beat

Listen to the sound we make with our knees.
tap fingers softly on knees to the beat

Listen to the sound we make with our teeth.
click teeth together

continue with other body parts

✔	**Fine Motor Skills**
✔	**Gross Motor Skills**
✔	**Listening Skills**

185

PAPER-BAG BLOCKS

STACKING BIG BLOCKS

SKILLSPOTLIGHT

Children enhance *their fine motor skills and their ability to discriminate among shapes and sizes when they explore and play with blocks. Most kids also love to practice stacking the blocks – then knocking them down, of course. That provides a good lesson in balance, as well as in cause and effect. And if your child builds a little fort or cave, having a private space that's just his size can bolster his emerging sense of identity.*

Cause & Effect	✔
Fine Motor Skills	✔
Problem Solving	✔
Size & Shape Discrimination	✔
Spatial Awareness	✔

AT THIS AGE, his hands may be too small to skill-fully maneuver heavy wooden blocks. But you can make large, lightweight blocks from paper bags and milk cartons that are both easy to handle and soft on impact.

• To make large blocks, fill a paper grocery bag to the brim with crumpled newspaper. Fold and tape the sides of the open end as if you were wrapping a present. Help your child decorate the oversize blocks using non-permanent markers, crayons, wrapping paper, or stickers.

• For smaller blocks, thoroughly rinse and dry empty milk cartons. Open the tops and vertically cut through the corner creases to create flaps. Tape the flaps shut and cover the cartons with colored construction paper or even contact paper with a brick motif (to create a "brick" house).

• Now let your kinder-contractor begin to build. Encourage him to stack the blocks as high as he can or to use them to create little forts. A couch or a table and sheets can provide additional walls and a roof.

• Also show him how to stack the small blocks on top of the big blocks to build a toddler-size tower. When it's time to disassemble the stack, take turns removing one block at a time, and count the blocks out loud as you remove them. Then create new structures with your little builder.

18 MONTHS
1 ½
AND UP

"Stack them high!"

PLAYING WITH PAPER BLOCKS helps
your young architect learn how to stack
objects and increases his understanding of size, shape, and balance.

SIZE WISE

SORTING OUT NESTING CUPS

YOUNG TODDLERS derive endless pleasure from taking objects out of a container and then trying to put them back again. Increase the complexity and fun of this type of activity by introducing your child to nesting objects, which require her to fit things together in a particular order.

• You can buy nesting containers at toy stores. Or use measuring spoons, mixing bowls, or cardboard boxes of different sizes for the same effect.

• Some toddlers do not yet have the manual dexterity to get the objects to nest or to pull them apart again. Start out slowly by introducing your child to this activity with only two or three nesting cups that vary dramatically in size. Demonstrate how the items fit within each other. You may need to show her several times, but eventually she'll be able to help you; then she'll figure out how to nest the objects on her own.

• Gradually add to the number of nesting objects once she has mastered fitting the first few cups or bowls together.

NESTING BOWLS TOGETHER teaches your toddler some important lessons about size differences while satisfying her curiosity about your shiny kitchenware.

RESEARCH REPORT

A toddler's ability *to sift through a jumble of cups and bowls and sort them into piles by size or shape demonstrates the dawning of logical reasoning. As exciting as it is to see a child master the simple but important concepts of same and different, it's obviously still a long journey to the type of sophisticated thinking associated with higher forms of logic. Jonas Langer, a psychologist at the University of California at Berkeley, notes that a child's logical powers make a big jump in complexity between the ages of four and eight, but she isn't able to truly comprehend notions of abstract symbolism until she reaches age eleven or so.*

189

HIDE YOUR EYES

SINGING THE PEEKABOO GAME

 to the *tune* of **"The Farmer in the Dell"**

**Can you hide your eyes,
can you hide your eyes?
Yes you can, you surely can,
you can hide your eyes.**
cover your eyes with your hands

**Can you hide your nose,
can you hide your nose?
Yes you can, you surely can,
you can hide your nose.**
cover your nose with your hands

**Can you hide your feet,
can you hide your feet?
Yes you can, you surely can,
you can hide your feet.**
cover your feet with your hands

*continue with chin, knees, toes,
elbows, ears, and so on*

Body Awareness	✔
Creative Movement	✔
Language Development	✔

190

THIS SINGALONG takes a toddler favorite — the peekaboo game — and applies it to several parts of your child's body. In turn, this helps her learn the words for many of her body parts as well as how to sing along with others.

• Kick off the "Can You Hide Your Eyes?" song with the names of some easy body parts, such as eyes, nose, feet, and toes. Then graduate to less familiar words, like elbows, knees, chin, and neck.

• Make a few mistakes once in a while to see if she catches them — cover your knees when you say "toes," for instance, or cover her knees instead of yours. She'll be amused by these silly contradictions.

YOUR CHILD GETS TO PLAY peekaboo while singing when you add these new lyrics to an old, familiar tune.

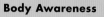

SHAKE IT UP, BABY!

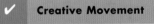

EXPERIMENTING WITH SOUND

INTRODUCE YOUR CURIOUS CHILD to new sounds and rhythms by supplying her with maracas or other percussion instruments (available in most toy stores). Or create your own musicmakers by filling a few plastic bottles with rice, dried beans, or pennies. Close the lids tightly and seal them with packaging tape to avoid any spillage (items under 1¾ inches, or 4.5 cm, in diameter are choking hazards). Begin by shaking each instrument, then pass it to your toddler, commenting on the unique sound it makes. Play a selection of familiar songs with different tempos and encourage her to make music and move her body to the beat.

A FEW HANDMADE INSTRUMENTS and a good song are all your toddler needs to let the rhythm move her.

SKILLSPOTLIGHT

Playing with musicmakers *stimulates auditory reflexes and nurtures a child's innate sense of rhythm, both of which are fundamental to language development. Identifying various kinds of sounds helps train the ear to recognize pitch and volume, while dancing and shaking or playing the instruments will encourage creative expression. If you make your own maracas, provide your child with additional tactile stimulation by allowing her to feel the rice, beans, or pennies before you put them in the bottles (but make sure she doesn't try to eat them).*

✔ **Creative Movement**

✔ **Listening Skills**

✔ **Rhythm Exploration**

✔ **Sensory Exploration**

191

SAND SKILLS

MAKING DESIGNS IN THE DIRT

SKILLSPOTLIGHT

Sand is wonderful *for artistic explorations because it allows a toddler to safely wallow in the medium from head to toe. Grasping and releasing the sand and using tools to manipulate it also exercise his fine motor skills and stimulate his sense of touch.*

Creative Expression	✔
Fine Motor Skills	✔
Tactile Stimulation	✔

IF YOUR CHILD ENJOYS THIS ACTIVITY, also try Nature Art, page 206. ▶

ZEN MASTERS DO IT. Bulldozers do it. And toddlers can do it, too. Whether you're at the beach, on a playground, or in a backyard sandbox, making designs in the sand is absorbing, creative, and entertaining. It also provides a great way to combine artistic endeavors with healthy outdoor play.

• Gather a variety of tot-size tools, including sand toys (plastic buckets, shovels, and molds), kitchen utensils (spatulas, wooden spoons, and plastic containers), and garden tools (watering cans and miniature rakes).

• Pour water over the sand to make a more pliable palette.

• Show your child how to use the tools to make designs. He can draw a rake through the sand, for instance, to create straight or wavy rows of lines. Or press a pie pan into the sand to make a big circle. Use empty yogurt containers and wet sand to add towers and turrets.

• Show your toddler how he can erase his creations by simply running his hands over the sand or by dumping a bucket of water on top of his mini masterpieces. Then let him wipe out and recreate his sand structures and patterns as many times as he likes.

MOST TODDLERS ARE THRILLED to play in a pile of sand; you can add to their fun by showing them how to make designs with sand toys and kitchen utensils.

18 MONTHS
$1\frac{1}{2}$
AND UP

PHOTO FUN

PUTTING NAMES TO FACES

SKILLSPOTLIGHT

Your toddler picks up *the rules of grammar by hearing your speech patterns. But she can't learn who Auntie is or what an ostrich looks like just by listening. She needs a picture to put a face to a name. This activity aids in expanding her vocabulary, which in turn helps her organize and share her memories.*

MAKING YOUR OWN

Tape or glue photos to playing cards or index cards. For extra protection from enthusiastic little hands, laminate the cards at a copy or framing shop. To hang, use tape or large magnets; avoid thumbtacks and small magnets.

IT MAY SEEM like your toddler has nothing but a Be Here Now (or Give It to Me Now) perspective on life. But she's been able to store and retrieve memories since she was about six months old. Now she's driven to remember and practice saying the names of people and objects around her. This flash-card activity is a means of memorizing while having some fun.

• Tape or glue photos of family members and friends to index cards (this will enable your child to pick them up more easily). Point to someone in a picture and say the person's name. Pretty soon she'll be calling out their names even before you do.

• Glue these photos to a piece of construction paper and laminate it for a personalized place mat.

• Using photos cut out of magazines, make cards depicting appealing things that aren't already in her daily life, such as an anteater, giraffe, or helicopter. Hang the cards at eye level (on the refrigerator, for example) and point them out to her often.

• Attach stories to the images so your toddler will have an easier time remembering them. You can say "We made cookies with Grandma, didn't we?" or "Rob has a big dog at his house, doesn't he?" This helps her learn how to tell stories, and it shows her that people are interested in them. It also helps her mentally process familiar events.

Language Development	✔
Visual Discrimination	✔
Visual Memory	✔

194

"Where's your uncle?"

HELP YOUR CHILD sharpen her memory skills by filling her world with images of familiar faces and intriguing objects.

195

THE MAGIC OF MUSIC

THE PASSION for music is a universal human trait, a gift parents from every culture instinctively bestow on their children. We coo lullabies as babies drift off to sleep, clap as toddlers make their first wobbly forays onto the living-room dance floor, and play endless games of patty-cake with our youngsters. Which is a good thing: recent studies, such as the one outlining the much-publicized Mozart effect detailed on page 233, suggest that exposure to music has far-reaching intellectual benefits that go beyond imparting a sense of melody and rhythm.

Mark Tramo, a neuroscientist at Harvard Medical School, explains that the same mental pathways used to process music also seem to serve as conduits for language, math, and abstract reasoning. "This means that exercising the brain through music strengthens other cognitive skills," Dr. Tramo concludes. The governor of Georgia, among many others, found this evidence so compelling he decided to send every baby born in Georgia home from the hospital with a recording of classical music.

This book includes simple and enjoyable suggestions for filling your child's world with the sound of music, from the tape-recorded parent-and-child duets on page 182 to the percussion games on page 210. Many of the activities link movement with music, which helps your toddler assimilate language and rhythm, develop coordination, and heighten body awareness. Complement these exercises by listening to a variety of music — while driving, eating, or doing chores, for example — and you'll further enhance her auditory senses and broaden her musical horizons. Don't feel you have to play classical music: introduce your child to the tunes you enjoy, and your pleasure will only make her more receptive to the value and power of all music. ■

196

18 MONTHS
1½
AND UP

TAMBOURINE TIME

MAKING MERRY MUSIC

THE TAMBOURINE IS MUSIC to your toddler's ears, arms, fingers, toes, and just about any other body part. Give him a tambourine and encourage him to shake it and tap it to the beat of his favorite songs — or to accompany you if you play an instrument. Move around as you play. Experiment with tambourines of different sizes: how do the sounds of large and small ones compare? How does the sound change when you shake the tambourine hard, then tap it gently? The two of you can delight in each other's musical discoveries.

SKILLSPOTLIGHT

Simple musical instruments *offer toddlers a rich variety of activities that both stimulate and fine-tune auditory and tactile senses. As children play and listen, they begin to discriminate among different rhythms and types of sounds. And a tambourine, which can be either tapped or shaken, reinforces what toddlers are already discovering: that the world is full of unique and varied sounds — sounds they not only can recognize but can produce themselves.*

✔	**Eye-Hand Coordination**
✔	**Listening Skills**
✔	**Rhythm Exploration**
✔	**Social Skills**

THE JINGLE and the jangle of a tambourine can teach a toddler a lot about sounds.

197

CRAYON CREATIONS

ARTWORK ON A GRAND SCALE

SKILLSPOTLIGHT

Grasping and using a crayon *builds fine motor skills and eye-hand coordination. It also can help a child learn to identify colors. More important, letting him express himself by choosing his colors and scribbling in whatever way he pleases allows him to give color and shape to his budding sense of identity. Discussing what the two of you are doing as you draw helps cement concepts in his memory and develop his communication skills.*

Concept Development	✔
Fine Motor Skills	✔
Social Skills	✔
Visual Memory	✔

E VEN CHILDREN as young as eighteen months are thrilled to put crayon and pen to paper. It can be hard for them to aim, however, and difficult to understand that the crayons or markers need to stay inside the paper's edges (and not on the table or floor). Rather than fence him in with standard letter-size paper, let your child spread his artistic wings to create mural-size artwork.

• Clear a large area on the floor and tape down poster-size sheets of paper. Sit next to your toddler, hand him some non-permanent markers or crayons, and encourage him to scribble on the paper. You may have to show him how at first, but once he gets going, he won't want to stop.

• Talk about what you're doing as you draw. When he picks up a crayon, tell him what color it is. Encourage him to use different colors and praise whatever marks he makes on the paper.

• With an older child, ask him to describe what he is drawing. If he's drawing a circle or square, for example, identify the shape and explain that it's round like a ball or square like a box. Control your desire to help him make perfect shapes. His drawings may look like only a bunch of squiggly lines to you, but they're masterpieces to him.

IF YOUR CHILD ENJOYS THIS ACTIVITY, also try Play With Clay, page 254. ▶

OVERSIZE CRAYONS and markers are easily gripped in the chubby fingers of your artist-in-the-making. Watch to see if he already has a favorite color!

18 MONTHS
1½
AND UP

199

COUNT WITH ME

YOUR TODDLER is always happy to bounce on your knee and hear you sing, but songs and chants that emphasize counting add educational fun. While your child will love just to listen to you, she'll also begin to recognize numbers. Repetition reinforces the learning, so sing an encore or two.

FIVE LITTLE RAINDROPS

Five little raindrops falling from a cloud,
wiggle fingers on one hand downward
the first one said,
  "My, the thunder's loud."
  hold up one finger; cover ears

  The second one said,
  "It's so cold tonight."
  hold up two fingers; shiver and hug body

The third one said,
"Oh, the lightning's so bright."
hold up three fingers; cover eyes

The fourth one said,
"Listen to the wind blow."
hold up four fingers; cup hand at ear

The fifth one said,
"Look, I'm turning into snow."
hold up five fingers; float fingers down

So down they tumbled through the cold winter's night,
roll arms downward in front of body
and turned all the earth to a frosty, snowy white.

COUNTING RAINDROPS, caterpillars, and crayons is a fun way to introduce your child to the concept of numbers.

THE CATERPILLAR

One little caterpillar crawled on my shoe.
wiggle finger like a worm on a shoe

Along came another and then there were two.
show two fingers

Two little caterpillars crawled on my knee.
wiggle two fingers on knee

Along came another and then there were three.
show three fingers

Three little caterpillars crawled on the floor.
walk three fingers across the floor

Along came another and then there were four.
show four fingers

Four little caterpillars all crawled away.
walk four fingers across the floor

They will all turn into butterflies one fine day!
flap your arms like a butterfly

TEN LITTLE CRAYONS

 to the *tune* of **"Ten Little Indians"**

**One little, two little, three little crayons,
four little, five little, six little crayons,
seven little, eight little, nine little crayons,
ten little crayons in a box.**
*hold up one finger for each crayon
as you count them*

Take out a red one and draw a big circle.
draw a circle with your finger

Take out a blue one and draw a straight line.
draw a straight line

Take out a yellow one and draw a little triangle.
draw a triangle

Then put them back in the box!
pretend to replace them in the crayon box

201

CEREAL CHALLENGE

GETTING TO THE CONTENTS

SKILLSPOTLIGHT

This is a deceptively simple *activity that promotes problem-solving techniques and demonstrates the concepts behind in and out as well as the principle of cause and effect. Once your child has mastered this challenge, raise the stakes with this visual memory game: take three small plastic containers such as bottles and hide a cereal bit in one of them. Mix them up, then urge her to find the one with the cereal (also see Magic Cups, page 247).*

Cause & Effect	✔
Concept Development	✔
Fine Motor Skills	✔
Problem Solving	✔

FIND A CLEAN, unbreakable small-mouthed bottle (a baby bottle or water bottle works well). Drop some of your toddler's favorite cereal or snack into it. Show your toddler the cereal in the open bottle and ask her to get it out. Allow her to experiment, but if she becomes overly frustrated, demonstrate how to tip the bottle over. Increase the challenge by lightly screwing on the top or asking her to drop the cereal back into the bottle. To further fine-tune her motor skills, try this with a variety of containers that have different types of lids.

BOTTOMS UP! There's nothing like a snack to motivate your budding genius— just watch how quickly she catches on.

SHAPE TO FIT

18 MONTHS
1½
AND UP

PUZZLING OUT A SOLUTION

WHICH SHAPES GO WHERE? Toddlers love a mystery, and this is one they can solve with some help from you. Use a shape-sorter toy or cut out three or four shapes on the top and sides of some sturdy cardboard boxes. (Make sure the shapes are about the same size so the triangle won't fit into the hole for the circle, for instance.) Ask your toddler to drop the shapes into the matching holes. Demonstrate the activity to get your child started, then let your young detective work on this visual mystery at her own pace.

MATCHING UP SHAPES teaches more than geometry; a child also learns how to solve new challenges.

SKILLSPOTLIGHT

The ability to classify *as well as discriminate among sizes and shapes is a fundamental skill that not only helps toddlers make sense of the world but prepares them for activities they'll encounter in play groups, camps, and preschool. Sorting, grasping, and fitting shapes promotes the development of fine motor skills and eye-hand coordination, which will in turn aid toddlers as they practice using forks and spoons, manipulating toys, and coloring. It may take some time before your child is able to easily discriminate among shapes, but most children this age enjoy practicing.*

✔	**Classifying Skills**
✔	**Eye-Hand Coordination**
✔	**Fine Motor Skills**
✔	**Size & Shape Discrimination**

203

POINT OUT THE PARTS

TALKING ABOUT THE BODY

SKILLSPOTLIGHT

Identifying and repeating *the names of specific body parts plays a role in language development; not only is your child learning to match your real nose to the word "nose," she's also feeling what a nose is by touching it or sniffing with it. The resulting physical sensations increase her awareness of her body and her body parts.*

Body Awareness	✔
Concept Development	✔
Language Development	✔
Listening Skills	✔

LABELING BODY PARTS is an important first step in your child's sense of herself as a separate person. This simple activity aids the process of self-discovery, which begins at the end of the first year of life and blossoms in the second. Learning and saying the names of body parts sharpens your toddler's verbal skills and memory, and increases her awareness of her body.

• To start, sit facing your child and touch her nose. Then take her finger in your hand and guide it to your nose. Say "nose" several times as you tap her finger on your nose. Then ask her to point to her own nose. Continue with other body parts, such as head, arm, leg, and foot. It may take her awhile to distinguish between "Mommy's nose" and "baby's nose"– that's natural. But eventually this will become a favorite game of hers and one that gives her a sense of accomplishment.

• If she has the verbal skills to say some of the names, ask her to repeat them as you point to them. Or initiate a movement game that shows her how to shake her head, stomp her foot, and wiggle her toes.

◀ *If your child enjoys this activity,* *also try Hide Your Eyes, page 190.*

KNOWING THE DIFFERENCE between Mommy's hair and her own mouth is a major milestone for a proud pointer. Next, talk about how her hands are small and yours are big.

PRESSING BACKYARD TREASURES
between contact paper is a creative
way to cultivate a love of the outdoors.

NATURE ART

CREATING A NATURAL COLLAGE

TODDLERS LOVE THE OUTDOORS, love to collect things, and love to dabble in the arts — as you've no doubt noticed with your child's oatmeal finger paintings at breakfast time or perhaps her crayon murals. Nurture this trio of passions by helping your toddler create a collage of natural elements.

• Take her on a walk in your backyard, a park, or the woods and collect small leaves, flowers, grass, sticks, feathers, and whatever else she finds that appeals to her (and is safe to handle).

• Use the outing as a time to expose your child to some new words and concepts by talking about what you find ("See this feather? That's from a blue jay." "Look, the flowers are turned toward the sun.").

• Once you're home, place a piece of clear contact paper, sticky side up, on top of a cookie sheet with a rim. Tape each corner of the contact paper to the cookie sheet to keep the paper from sticking to your hands.

• Help your child arrange her outdoor treasures on the contact paper.

• Place another piece of transparent contact paper, sticky side down, over the first one to help preserve your toddler's work of art.

• Hang the collage in a window, on the refrigerator, even in your child's room . . . anywhere she can proudly showcase her creation.

SKILLSPOTLIGHT

Letting your child choose *her own objects (a red flower versus a yellow one, for instance) and arrange them herself helps her identify and express her personal preferences. Talking to her about nature as you explore the outdoors encourages her to notice and describe the world. And the task of applying objects to paper – especially a sticky contact sheet – helps enhance her fine motor skills.*

✔	**Creative Expression**
✔	**Eye-Hand Coordination**
✔	**Fine Motor Skills**
✔	**Language Development**

207

WATER THE PLANTS

A MUSICAL MIME

to the *tune* of **"The Mulberry Bush"**

**This is the way we
water the plants,**
*put one hand on hip and bend
the other like a curved spout*
**water the plants,
water the plants.**

**This is the way we
water the plants
whenever they get dry.**

**We water the plants
so they will grow,**
*crouch down on the floor,
then slowly stand up*
**they will grow,
they will grow.**

**We water the plants
so they will grow
way up to the sky.**
raise your hands skyward

| **Balance** | ✔ |
| **Coordination** | ✔ |

THIS GARDENING SONG will teach your tyke a fundamental lesson about nature: that plants need water to grow! Show your child how to tip way over as he "pours" the water from his "spout." That's good balance practice. If he likes rowdier play, pick him up and tip him over instead. Reinforce the gardening lesson by asking him to help you water real plants, either inside or outside. He'll enjoy both participating in your chores (see Copycat, page 290) and nurturing living things.

TWISTING LIKE A SPOUT gives your little one a handle on what makes gardens grow.

18 MONTHS
1½
AND UP

SURPRISE!

UNWRAPPING TOY TREASURES

FOR TODDLERS, the wrapping paper on a present is at least as fun as the gift itself. They love the brightly colored paper, the noise it makes when they crinkle it, and the challenge of discovering what's inside. Your child can enjoy this activity any day of the year if you gather several of his favorite toys and wrap them loosely in colorful paper (no tape) while he watches.

Show him one package at a time, asking, "What's inside the paper?" Let him remove the wrapping — but lend a helping hand if he gets frustrated. Wad up the paper while commenting on the sound it makes and how it feels.

THE ACT OF UNWRAPPING stimulates the senses and helps develop coordination.

SKILLSPOTLIGHT

Unwrapping an object *requires solving problems and having nimble fingers. Playing with different patterns and textures stimulates a child's visual, tactile, and auditory senses, especially when the paper crinkles or pops as he handles it.*

✔ **Coordination**

✔ **Problem Solving**

✔ **Sensory Exploration**

✔ **Tactile Discrimination**

209

RHYTHM TIME

FUN WITH A DRUM

Your child is born *with an innate sense of rhythm. But learning to pound out a beat – especially while practicing with you – lets her see how it fits into music, dance, and other rhythmic activities. Drumming also enhances her eye-hand coordination, and learning to vary the pace and volume fine-tunes her muscle control.*

MAKING YOUR OWN

Creating a drum is as simple as turning over a saucepan or wooden bowl. Try metal, plastic, and wooden spoons for varying sound effects; use different-size containers to create varying pitches (the smaller they are, the higher the pitch).

Cause & Effect	✔
Creative Expression	✔
Listening Skills	✔
Rhythm Exploration	✔

YOUR CHILD ALREADY KNOWS how to make plenty of noise by banging her spoon on the table, clapping her hands, and pounding on the door she wants opened. You can direct this energy toward more musical pursuits – as well as encourage her sense of rhythm – by showing her how to bang out a beat with a drum.

- Buy a drum and mallet, or make your own. Sit down with your child and show her how to hit the drum with either a mallet or her hand. Demonstrate how to hit the drum softly, then loudly. Vary the pace of the drumming so she experiences fast beats as well as slow ones.

- Put on some lively music and demonstrate how to drum to the beat. Don't expect her to follow the music exactly – that will come when she's older. Sway back and forth, tap your foot, clap your hands, and toss your head from side to side to show her other ways of expressing rhythm. Or get your own drum and pound out a noisy duet.

IF YOUR CHILD ENJOYS THIS ACTIVITY, also try Shake It Up, Baby!, page 191.

SHOW YOUR LITTLE DRUMMER GIRL
the different sounds she can make, then
let her march to her own beat.

"Bang, bang the drum!"

TODDLER PARADE

MAKING A SPECIAL DAY WITH EVERYDAY TOYS

SKILLSPOTLIGHT

This is the very beginning *of fantasy play: they are pretending to be a member of the parade and they're mentally converting their toys (and you) into appropriate props. Walking or marching to music can help them learn rhythm. And they'll develop new levels of coordination by figuring out how to pull their pretend-parade behind them.*

Creative Expression	✔
Fine Motor Skills	✔
Gross Motor Skills	✔

EVERYONE LOVES A PARADE — but you don't have to wait for a holiday or struggle with crowds to let your toddler participate in one. Instead, create a pint-size parade in your own home, complete with music, celebrities (albeit fuzzy ones), and an emcee. Make your child the grand marshal of the event.
• Help her collect her wheeled toys in the "staging grounds" (for example, your living room). Tie the toys together with short lengths of string so she can pull the makeshift contraption behind her. If you have a toy wagon, prop stuffed animals inside to serve as famous folk. To get really fancy, decorate the "floats" with streamers and ribbons. You could even make confetti!

NOTHING CAN RAIN on their personal parade when they have their rolling elephants, horses, and lion marching right along behind them.

212

18 MONTHS 1½ AND UP

• When your toddler gets a little older, play lively marching music, outfit yourself with a drum (a spoon and a pot will do) or a fake baton, and parade around with your child in tow. She probably won't be able to march and pull her toys at the same time, so pull the floats for her while she practices stepping high and swinging her little arms.

RESEARCH REPORT

In studies conducted *in the United States and Britain, psychologists Anthony Pellegrini and Peter K. Smith showed that children instinctively seem to understand the importance of play and freedom of movement. When their free play was restricted for a period of time, the "deprivation led to increased levels of play when opportunities for play were resumed," the psychologists concluded. In other words, when finally let loose, the kids tried to make up for lost playtime.*

◀ *If your child enjoys this activity, also try Band on the Run, page 170.*

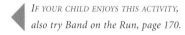

PLAYING WITH SIBLINGS

WHEN PLAYING one-on-one with a toddler, you can easily adapt to your child's needs and desires. But when a sibling is introduced into the group, the dynamics change dramatically, calling for a parent to exercise a bit more imagination and diplomacy.

Several factors complicate the situation: toddlers aren't always keen on sharing their parents' attention, even with a beloved brother or sister. If there's more than a two-year gap in ages, just finding an activity that suits both children can be a challenge. Then there are different play styles to consider: one child may be the quiet type who prefers to play alone with blocks, while his dynamo of a sister likes nothing more than to help him build block towers – before knocking them down. No wonder a session of family fun can leave you feeling more like a referee in an extra-fierce World Wrestling Entertainment match than a play partner.

Still, there are many ways to ensure smoother, more enjoyable play sessions. Taking into account the children's ages and personalities, devise activities that will be fun for both and accommodate different play styles. Art projects such as drawing with sidewalk chalk or painting, for instance, can be enjoyed by toddlers and young school-age children alike. Going to a playground outfitted with a variety of equipment allows children to play together for a while, and then pursue individual interests. And don't forget to stock up on duplicate toys and supplies when possible; having two sets of watercolors and two rainbow-colored balls has saved many a parent from sibling meltdown. It's also important to dole out attention in fairly equal measures. While it's natural to pay more attention to the younger child, as she might need more help, remember to offer words of praise or encouragement to the older sibling. ■

BABY BASKETBALL

SLAM-DUNKING A FAVORITE GAME

GATHER A FEW medium-size balls and place them in a large container such as a laundry basket, cardboard box, or plastic bowl. Show your child how to empty the balls onto the floor, then demonstrate how to drop the balls one by one into the basket. Initially, your toddler may enjoy simply putting the balls in the basket and taking them back out. When he's ready, have him stand back and try throwing the balls into the basket. Increase the challenge by placing a few containers around the room, then urge your athlete to aim toward a different one each time.

ALL YOUR YOUNG DRIBBLER needs to practice his eye-hand coordination and motor skills is a ball, a basket, and an enthusiastic coach!

SKILLSPOTLIGHT

When your child *practices aiming, he improves his eye-hand coordination and gross motor skills. And if you count the balls out loud as your toddler throws them into the containers, you'll help lay the foundation for understanding numbers. Whether your child is tossing the ball into a basket or at you, actively participate by gently throwing the ball back to him. Encourage him to take another (more difficult) fundamental step: learning to catch.*

✔	**Eye-Hand Coordination**
✔	**Gross Motor Skills**
✔	**Social Skills**

215

THE NOBLE DUKE OF YORK

A CLASSIC SONG AND MIME

SKILL SPOTLIGHT

Your toddler *is beginning to form a clearer sense of himself as an object in space. This song game – while fun to play with a parent – helps him learn the meanings of spatial words, such as "up," "down," and "over." And while your child may not be quite old enough to tell right from left, he'll get the idea, at least, that those words refer to something other than straight ahead.*

Concept Development	✔
Language Development	✔
Spatial Awareness	✔

IF YOUR CHILD ENJOYS THIS ACTIVITY, also try The Choo-Choo Train, page 220.

YOUR CHILD'S UNDERSTANDING of the concepts of space and movement increases slowly but surely in the toddler years. If your child loved lap songs as a baby, he'll get a big kick out of this more advanced version, which teaches him just some of the ways he can move about in the world.

• As with all song games, enunciating the sounds clearly and emphasizing the corresponding movements help teach your toddler the meaning of the most important words. Those emphases also create a song with more drama and vigor, which makes it more exciting for the two of you.

• As your toddler gets older, he can sing this song standing on the floor instead of sitting on your knees. Try marching during the first stanza, then stretching up and crouching down in the second stanza. With the third stanza, have him drop to the floor and lie on his back, then gently push his legs left, right, and up in the air.

18 MONTHS 1½ AND UP

THIS FUN TUNE – bolstered by Mommy's bouncy movements – helps your little duke learn about moving up and down.

**The noble Duke of York,
he had ten thousand men,**
*bounce child on your knees,
facing outward*
**he marched them up to
the top of the hill,**
*march your legs upward with
child still on knees*
**and he marched them
down again.**
*march your legs downward with
child still on knees*

**And when you're up,
you're up.**
raise both legs
**And when you're down,
you're down.**
drop both legs

**And when you're only
halfway up,**
*raise both legs halfway
up and pause*
**you're neither
up nor down.**
move legs up and down quickly

He rolled them over left,
lean to the left
he rolled them over right,
lean to the right
**he rolled them over
upside down,**
*lie backward with child lying
on top of you*
oh, what a funny sight!
return to original position

217

TUBE TRICKS

WHERE DOES THE BALL GO?

MAKING YOUR OWN

You can find tubes of all sizes at hardware stores, hobby stores, art galleries, photo shops, and the post office. Any soft balls that fit in the tube will work: tennis balls, racquet balls, or balls made of cloth, soft rubber, or foam.

I N O N E E N D and out the other. It seems simple to us, but to a toddler it's like playing hide-and-seek with a ball, which is sure to puzzle and thrill her. Even when she's mastered the mystery ("Where did the ball go? There it is!"), she'll want to play this game again and again.

• Start with a wide plastic or cardboard tube and a supply of tennis, racquet, or other soft balls. Put the balls in one end of the tube, tilt the tube so they roll down inside it, and have her retrieve them from the other end. Repeat several times. Then have her put the balls in and you catch them.

• Increase the complexity by using balls of different sizes. Which ones fit in the tube? Which ones don't? Be sure to choose balls that are at least 1¾ inches (4.5 cm) in diameter so they do not pose a choking hazard.

• You can turn this activity into a coordination exercise by asking her to catch a ball as it's falling out of the tube. She waits at the bottom end of the tube, and as the ball pops out, she tries to grab it. The smaller the ball, the greater the challenge.

IF YOUR CHILD ENJOYS THIS ACTIVITY, also try Baby Basketball, page 215.

Cause & Effect	✔
Fine Motor Skills	✔
Size & Shape Discrimination	✔

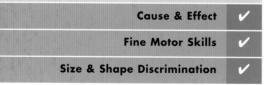

A **CLEAR TUBE** lets her watch the blue balls roll all the way from top to bottom; an opaque tube will add an element of surprise to the game.

18 MONTHS 1½ AND UP

THE CHOO-CHOO TRAIN

AN EXCURSION IN RHYME

sit facing your child and hold both of her hands

Here comes the choo-choo train, coming down the track. First it's going forward, then it's going back.
pull one hand toward you while pushing the other toward your child; continue to alternate

Now the bell is ringing: ding, ding, ding!
ring imaginary bell

Now the whistle blows: whoo, whoo, whoo!
pull imaginary whistle cord

What a lot of noise it makes
cover both of your ears
everywhere it goes!

Language Development	✔
Rhythm Exploration	✔

TODDLERS DON'T NEED a melody to sense rhythm: they can feel beats with simple chants. When you add appealing rhymes, fun movements, an ever-friendly train theme, and an enthusiastic parent, you've got an activity that will keep your little one chugging merrily along.

• While you chant "Here Comes the Choo-Choo Train," play up the rhythm so your toddler can hear it and mimic it with her body. Ham up the movements, too. Emphasizing the gestures will help your eager engineer understand the meaning of the accompanying words.

THIS CHANTING game teaches your little conductor to feel a beat and understand the basics of forward and backward motion.

TANTALIZING TEXTURES

18 MONTHS
1½
AND UP

A BOOK OF SENSATIONS

HE'S ALREADY DETERMINED to get his hands on everything in (and out of) sight, including dollops of jam, dead bugs, and months-old cereal bits. Let his fingers experience the world safely by introducing him to a book filled with tactile adventures. You can buy a texture book or make your own.

• To create the book, collect a variety of materials, such as cloth, burlap, foil, wax paper, and bubble wrap. Glue a large square of each material onto cardboard or construction paper. Then tie or tape the sheets together.

• When you explore the book with your toddler, describe the different sensations you both are feeling.

SKILLSPOTLIGHT

A texture book *lets your toddler discover a variety of different materials and helps him learn concepts such as rough, smooth, bumpy, and even squishy. The book can also give your child the chance to express his preferences: Does he like the scratchy feel of burlap? Or does he prefer the crinkliness of the foil?*

✔	**Language Development**
✔	**Tactile Discrimination**
✔	**Tactile Stimulation**

BOOK PAGES made of unusual textures, such as fine sandpaper or fake fur, let your child explore the world from the safety of your lap.

221

MAGNET MAGIC

PLAYING WITH TOYS THAT STICK

SKILLSPOTLIGHT

Grasping and moving *magnets helps build fine motor skills – the ones he'll need for drawing, completing puzzles, fastening little buttons, and, eventually, writing. Discussing these intriguing magnets helps him learn to distinguish among colors and sizes and helps expand his vocabulary, while making a magnet "disappear" exercises his visual memory.*

Counting Concepts	✔
Fine Motor Skills	✔
Size & Shape Discrimination	✔
Visual Memory	✔

MAKING YOUR OWN

Create personalized magnets by gluing or taping photos of family members onto inexpensive, flat magnets. Or attach photos, drawings, or magazine pictures of your child's favorite animals. Photo stores carry magnetized photo frames, as well.

MANY CHILDREN display their manual dexterity by pulling magnets off the refrigerator – and then crowing delightedly over their finds. You can make magnets even more fun by using them for a variety of games that engage your child's eyes and memory, as well as his curious fingers.

• Gather several colorful magnets and place them on a metal cookie sheet (note: magnets won't adhere to aluminum sheets). Use magnets with images of objects, such as animals, flowers, food, storybook characters, numbers, and vehicles. Avoid magnets that are smaller than 1¾ inches (4.5 cm) in diameter because they pose a choking hazard. And choose magnets with well-defined edges so your child can pick them up easily.

• Ask your toddler to take the magnets off the sheet – then ask him to put them back on. Talk to him about the colors, sizes, and characters he sees on the magnets. Encourage him to move them around to create his own design. With an older toddler, remove a magnet from the sheet and ask him to guess which one is missing.

IF YOUR CHILD ENJOYS THIS ACTIVITY, also try Tantalizing Textures, page 221.

YOUR TODDLER IS FAR TOO YOUNG to understand magnetic attraction, but learning that certain objects adhere to a cookie sheet is the very beginning of scientific discovery.

223

18 MONTHS
1½
AND UP

OPEN SHUT THEM!

A TICKLING RHYME AND CHANT

Open shut them,
open and close fists
open shut them,
give a little clap, clap, clap!
clap three times

Open shut them,
open and close fists
open shut them,
put them in your lap, lap, lap!
pat lap three times

Creep them, crawl them,
slowly creep them,
right up to your chin, chin, chin!
walk fingers from chest to chin,
tickling your child along the way

Open wide your little mouth,
touch lips with a finger
but do not let them in!
quickly run fingers down to lap,
tickling your child along the way

Creative Expression	✔
Fine Motor Skills	✔
Language Development	✔

TODDLERS HAVE A GREAT LOVE
for their own little bodies — and the names of their own
little body parts. They also enjoy tickle and surprise games.
This chant gives your child a chance to show off her knowledge of her
body and at the same time play a creepy-crawly tickle game.
• Start out by demonstrating the chant's gestures
on yourself and see if
she can follow along.
If she seems confused,
do the fingerplay on her
instead — until she is
ready to copy you.

YOUR CHILD will enjoy
playing the creepy-crawly
game with her fingers —
especially when Mommy
is an active participant.

224

BEACH-BALL CATCH

24 MONTHS AND UP · 2

A TOSS-AND-CATCH BALL GAME

MOST TODDLERS are able to throw a ball before they can catch one. But they love trying to wrap their little arms around airborne balls, and with a healthy dose of patience and practice you can help your child learn the basics of catching. Start by rolling a ball to her and asking her to roll it back to you (see Pass the Ball, page 152). When she's ready to attempt catching, use a slightly deflated beach ball (it's easier for small hands to grasp).

• Kneel or sit a couple of feet apart and ask her to throw the beach ball to you. Demonstrate how to catch, then toss the ball to her and ask her to catch it. Once she accomplishes this (it will take a lot of practice), increase the distance between you, little by little.

YOUR CHILD will catch on more quickly if you show her how to grab the ball before you toss it her way.

SKILL SPOTLIGHT

Playing a game of catch with a toddler is a fun and simple exercise in socialization that builds gross motor skills and eye-hand coordination. Successful catches demand quick reflexes and good spatial awareness, which may take awhile for your toddler to achieve. By enthusiastically supporting your child in her attempts to catch, you are teaching her to appreciate being part of a game in a noncompetitive way.

✓ **Eye-Hand Coordination**

✓ **Gross Motor Skills**

✓ **Social Skills**

225

BALANCING ACT

STANDING TALL ON A BALANCE BEAM

SKILLSPOTLIGHT

Just like logs and low walls, *balance beams present an irresistible challenge to curious young children. As she perfects her walk along the beam, her ability to balance increases, and she develops crucial eye-foot coordination – skills that will help her as she moves from walking to running, jumping, hopping, skipping, and – who knows? – maybe even perfecting a gymnastic dismount.*

Balance	✔
Eye-Foot Coordination	✔
Spatial Awareness	✔

IF YOUR CHILD ENJOYS THIS ACTIVITY, also try Footstep Fun, page 241. ▶

ATTEMPTING TO BALANCE on narrow walkways is a natural and universal activity for young children, so you probably won't have to do much to encourage your child to try. You can find beams low enough to walk on safely at gyms, parks, and playgrounds. Demonstrate how to walk across, then hold your child's hand as she tries to walk slowly on the beam.

• If your toddler is reluctant at first, place a toy at the other end of the beam and encourage your young gymnast to hold your hand and walk across to retrieve it. Be sure she practices this balancing act above a soft or cushioned surface.

SHE'LL BE SUREFOOTED in no time with her favorite coach by her side for support.

226

PUPPET PLAY

24 MONTHS
2
AND UP

AN OLD-FASHIONED STAGE SHOW

CHILDREN ADORE PUPPETS because they're toys that seem to magically come to life. They'll love them even more when you put on a live, slapstick show. You can buy puppets – or just use brightly colored felt-tipped pens to draw a face on a sock or a bag. You can even tape ears or horns on your home-made puppet and glue "hair" made of yarn to its top.

• Make a stage by draping a blanket over the back of a chair or a safety gate – or position yourself behind a sofa. With one or two puppets, tell your child stories and sing songs. Use a different voice for each puppet.

• Ask your child questions with the puppets and encourage him to converse. Question him about his favorite foods, his special toys, or his mommy and daddy. And ask him to show the puppet his nose and toes – toddlers love to point these things out.

SKILLSPOTLIGHT

By the age of two, *your child is attributing all sorts of human traits to his toys; he considers them his best friends. By making puppet toys act more like humans, you stimulate his imagination. And by telling stories and conversing with him, you accelerate his back-and-forth conversational skills.*

✔ **Imagination**

✔ **Language Development**

✔ **Social Skills**

A BIG, FAT FROG and a polka-dotted duck can share some pretty funny stories with their little human friend.

227

TRAIN TRIPS

AN IMAGINARY LOCOMOTIVE

SKILLSPOTLIGHT

In this activity, *your little engineer enhances her upper body muscle coordination and learns to move with the rhythm of a chant. Puffing along as your pint-size passenger, she develops whole body coordination as well as balance – after all, it's hard to stay seated on Mommy when you're busy giggling like crazy. Role-playing also greases the gears of the imagination.*

Coordination	✔
Gross Motor Skills	✔
Imagination	✔
Social Skills	✔

YOU CAN HARNESS your child's abundant steam power by taking her on an imaginary train trip. Announce your destination ("First stop, Mommy's lap!"), pretend to pull the whistle ("Whoo whoo!"), then invite her to sit on your lap. As you chant "chug-a-chug-a-choo-choo," push her hands in a circle (like the rolling train wheels) or help her blow the whistle. Alternatively, you can both "chug" around the house ("Next stop, your bedroom!") with your child as the engine and you as the caboose.

• Pretend to navigate around curves by bending both of your bodies from side to side. Go through "tunnels" (don't forget to duck your heads!) and stop from time to time to let passengers off at the "depot."

• Sing a favorite train song or chant (see The Choo-Choo Train, page 220) while you chug around the house together.

• To help a toddler appreciate trains and enjoy this activity even more, take her to a real train station – or even the subway – and show your young conductor what it's like to ride the rails.

IF YOUR CHILD ENJOYS THIS ACTIVITY, also try Drive the Fire Truck, page 250. ▶

"Whoo whoo! All aboard!"

SHE'LL EXPAND her locomotor skills and blow off a good bit of steam in this vigorous lap game.

THE "NO" STAGE

A **BIG SHOCK** to first-time parents is the transformation of their easygoing, compliant infants into mercurial toddlers whose favorite word seems to be no – as in "no bananas," "no bath," and "no songs," even though they never seemed to mind these things before. As Dr. Benjamin Spock wrote in *Baby and Child Care,* "When you suggest something that doesn't appeal to them, they feel they must assert themselves. . . . Psychologists call it 'negativism.'" While admitting that this spell of negativism can test the resources of even the most patient parents, Spock also noted that this stage is an important signal that children are maturing into independent human beings who can think for themselves.

Being calm, cooperative, and reasonable with your toddler is one of the most effective ways to teach him to be a calm, cooperative, and reasonable person himself – but it will take time. Until he learns more self-control, you can expect temper tantrums when he doesn't get his way. It's best to ignore such behavior – if you can – to convey that he can't get what he wants in this unseemly manner. In *Raising Good Children,* developmental psychologist Thomas Lickona advises parents to keep toddlers happily busy, offer diversions when they get restless, and allow lots of free play in safe settings. He also recommends counting, such as saying, "Let's see if you can get in your chair by the time I count to ten." Another strategy is to present a child with alternatives. If he insists on wearing clothes that aren't appropriate for the weather, you could pick out two suitable outfits and say, "Which would you like to wear today?" Such maneuvers might seem transparent to adults, but they are wonderfully effective in making a headstrong toddler feel a measure of the control and freedom he so desires. ■

PONY RIDES

TAKING A LIVING-ROOM TROT

SHE'S FASCINATED by pictures of horses, but a wee bit wary of the real thing. Give her a leg up on balance skills by playing the pony part yourself. Get down on your hands and knees and let your child ride on your back or shoulders. Make sure she hangs on tight, and be ready to grab a leg if she starts sliding.

• If you want to add music to this activity, sing "Trot Little Pony" (see Silly Lap Songs, page 178, for the lyrics) or another of your toddler's favorite songs as you crawl around the room. To help her learn to adjust her balance, lower your upper body to the floor, raise it (not too high!), or wiggle from side to side.

GIDDYAP DADDY! You can start your little cowgirl's riding lessons early by doing some of the legwork in your living room.

SKILLSPOTLIGHT

Sure, a two-year-old *can walk pretty well. But that doesn't mean her balance is fully developed. As you crawl and wiggle your way through the house, your child is learning how to find and keep her center of gravity. She'll also be stretching her imagination by pretending she's riding a pretty pony – or perhaps a dashing steed.*

✔	**Balance**
✔	**Gross Motor Skills**
✔	**Imagination**

231

HEAD TO TOES

GENTLE GYM

touch the body part with both hands as you sing its name

Head, shoulders, knees, and toes.

Knees and toes!

Head, shoulders, knees, and toes.

Knees and toes!

Eyes and ears and mouth and nose, head, shoulders, knees, and toes.

Knees and toes!

Body Awareness	✔
Gross Motor Skills	✔
Listening Skills	✔
Rhythm Exploration	✔
Visual Memory	✔

YOU MAY REMEMBER this song from your own childhood, when you sang it at camp, in school, or with your friends or parents. It's also a great tune for helping toddlers learn – and remember – the names of body parts.

• Sing "Head, Shoulders, Knees, and Toes" to your child and place both hands on your body parts as you call out the name of each part.

• Keep singing the song over and over, increasing the tempo each time. You'll probably both get mixed up and a bit breathless toward the end – but that's part of the fun!

• Is your toddler having trouble keeping up? Try touching her body as you sing to help her learn how the words and motions fit together.

IF YOUR CHILD ENJOYS THIS ACTIVITY, also try Circle Songs, page 234. ▶

TOE-TOUCHING to the music puts your toddler in tune with her body parts — and her feel for the beat.

RESEARCH REPORT

Not only does music soothe *the savage breast, it seems to perk up the mind as well. Physicist Gordon Shaw and psychologist Frances Rauscher made worldwide head-lines in 1993 with a research project showing that college stu-dents who listened to Mozart's* Sonata for Two Pianos in D Major *for ten minutes before a test of their spatial-temporal reasoning ability averaged an eight- or nine-point jump in scores. This finding, along with other studies, so impressed Florida legislators that they enacted the "Beethoven's Babies" bill in 1998, which requires state-funded day care centers to play classical music for thirty minutes every day. While "Head, Shoulders, Knees, and Toes" is a far cry from Mozart, Rauscher believes any complex music (be it classical, jazz, or rock) might enhance brain development.*

233

CIRCLE SONGS

THESE PERENNIAL FAVORITES are a perfect choice when your toddler has the urge to move all around. Best of all, there's a camaraderie and joy that comes with circling, singing, and holding hands – whether with Mommy and Daddy or a few cherished friends.

RING AROUND THE ROSY

Ring around the rosy,
hold hands and walk in a circle
pocket full of posies,
ashes, ashes,
we all fall down!
fall to the ground

The cows are in the pasture,
remain seated in the circle
eating buttercups,
pretend to eat
thunder, lightning,
pound hands on the floor
we all stand up!
stand up quickly

THE MULBERRY BUSH

Here we go round the mulberry bush,
hold hands and walk in a circle
the mulberry bush,
the mulberry bush.
Here we go round the mulberry bush,
so early in the morning.

This is the way we clap our hands,
clap hands while standing in a circle
clap our hands,
clap our hands.
This is the way we clap our hands,
so early in the morning.

This is the way we stamp our feet . . .
This is the way we turn around . . .
This is the way we twist and shout . . .
This is the way we reach and stretch . . .
This is the way we run and run . . .
This is the way we sit right down . . .
This is the way we wash our face . . .

LOOBY LOO

Here we go looby loo,
hold hands and walk in a circle
here we go looby light,
here we go looby loo,
all on a Saturday night.
jump up with arms extended skyward

POP GOES THE WEASEL

All around the cobbler's bench,
hold hands and run in a circle
the monkey chased the weasel,
the monkey thought
it was all in fun,
POP goes the weasel!
jump up, then fall
to the ground

Up, down, all around:
Circle songs give your toddler a
dizzying array of tunes to move to
and supportive hands to hold.

235

SCARF TRICKS

CATCHING THE FLUTTERING FABRIC

SKILLSPOTLIGHT

A two-year-old *is biologically driven to practice gross motor movements of all kinds, such as running, kicking, jumping, and rolling. This activity gives her a new object with which to practice throwing and catching: a silky, fluttering scarf that is as engaging to watch as it is to touch.*

Eye-Foot Coordination	✔
Eye-Hand Coordination	✔
Gross Motor Skills	✔

SHE MAY HAVE almost mastered catching a rolling ball, a wobbling plastic lid, or the family cat. Here's something altogether different to challenge her eye-hand coordination. Gather some brightly colored, lightweight scarves. Scrunch up a few of them simultaneously in your hand and throw them high in the air, then ask your child to try to catch them as they float and flutter toward the ground. After a few rounds, let her throw some of the scarves while you take a turn at nabbing them midair. As she gets older, encourage her to spin around or clap her hands before catching the scarves.

PLUCKING A RAINBOW of color from the air is as visually stimulating as it is physically challenging—and fun!

236

RING-A-LING

FUN WITH PHONES

TODDLERS ARE DRAWN to telephones like bears are drawn to honey. But rather than shooing your two-year-old from your carefully programmed cordless telephone, give her a phone of her own. You can use a castoff from your basement, or buy a toy phone (some even have push buttons that beep).

Encourage her to use it by holding the receiver to her ear and asking simple questions, such as "What's your name?" "What are you doing today?" and "May I talk to your daddy, please?"

"THIS IS CHRISTINA. Can you visit today?" A pretend phone call with Grandpa or Auntie helps your budding socialite learn the give-and-take of conversation.

SKILLSPOTLIGHT

Learning to hold *a conversation, even if it's an imaginary one, helps children exercise their emerging language and social skills. This activity is also a useful way to introduce basic phone etiquette ("Who's calling, please?" or "I'm fine, thank you") before your toddler starts picking up your phone and talking to your callers.*

✔	**Creative Expression**
✔	**Language Development**
✔	**Self-Concept**
✔	**Social Skills**

IF YOUR CHILD ENJOYS THIS ACTIVITY, also try Doll Talk, page 258.

GOOD THROW! It may not be fun for the hippo bean-bag, but your little champ will be bowled over by this game of knock 'em down.

RESEARCHREPORT

In their book Magic Trees of the Mind, *neuroanatomist Marian Diamond and science reporter Janet Hopson stress the importance of spatial exercises, such as this bean-bag bowling activity, which help spur both physical and mental development. Spatial intelligence (which includes the ability to judge distance and dimensions), they point out, "is one of the most tangible, practical mental abilities," while spatial exercises are "one of the many ways for a child to have fun and . . . let the future in."*

24 MONTHS AND UP
2

BEANBAG BOWLING

LEARNING HOW TO THROW

WHETHER IT'S PUSHING his fork off his highchair tray or pulling your CDs off the shelves, your toddler delights in putting objects in motion — just to see what will happen (and often to see how you'll react). This is a natural way for toddlers to learn about cause and effect. It's also a good way for them to learn about concepts like gravity and force (not that they need to learn those words — at least not yet). If you're concerned with concepts such as object fragility, however, channel your child's curiosity about crashes into a game the two of you can play.

• Stack several tall, lightweight plastic bottles, cups, or empty cans. Show your child how to throw a beanbag animal to knock them down. (It will be easier for him to do this from a seated position.) Then take turns tossing the beanbags — but don't bother keeping score.

• Vary the activity by using different-size balls or even pincushions — without pins, of course — instead of beanbags. Also try seating your child at varying distances from the stack. He'll soon discover that he needs to throw with more force when he's farther away from his target.

• Once your baby bowler improves his game, ask him to toss the beanbags while standing. And to make the activity more fun for you, encourage him to collect the "pins" he has now learned to blast into all corners of the room!

SKILLSPOTLIGHT

Throwing beanbag toys or balls at targets helps toddlers develop their eye-hand coordination and adds to their understanding of cause and effect. This activity also helps your child learn to take turns, a skill he'll work on throughout his early years. Taking turns will be crucial to later social interactions, such as at school, when children need to share to get along with others.

✔	**Balance**
✔	**Cause & Effect**
✔	**Eye-Hand Coordination**
✔	**Gross Motor Skills**

239

WHO ARE WE?

PLAYING DRESS-UP

SKILLSPOTLIGHT

Most two-year-olds *have strong preferences when it comes to their clothing. And many are determined to dress themselves no matter how long it takes. This activity gives them the license to choose their clothes – and the luxury of dressing themselves at their leisure. Role-playing activities also act as dress rehearsals for social interactions later in life.*

Creative Expression	✔
Imagination	✔
Role-Playing	✔
Social Skills	✔

A PRINCESS, A COWBOY, a movie star . . . children love the costume dramas that dressing up inspires.

SHE STARTED TOYING with your scarves, hats, and soft sweaters when she first learned to grab; she headed for your closets as soon as she could crawl. Now it's time to let her go wild with her own wardrobe. Keep a variety of dress-up items on hand (garage sales and thrift stores are great, often inexpensive sources) and let your child don what she may to be whoever she pleases. Participate in the fun by asking her who she is that day, and invite some of her pals to join in on the act.

240

FOOTSTEP FUN

FOLLOWING THE FEET

EVER SINCE your toddler was a baby, he's been fascinated by his own feet, whether it's the taste of his toes or the look of his first walking shoes. Let him get a whole new view of his feet — as well as strong motor skills practice — by teaching him to follow his own footsteps. Trace the outline of the soles of his shoes onto colored pieces of paper. Cut out the foot shapes and glue them onto cardboard squares. Place the squares on the floor to form a path, then encourage your trailblazer to place his feet inside each of the silhouettes.

BY ASKING YOUR LITTLE ONE to follow a path of colorful footprints, you provide stepping stones to greater coordination.

SKILL SPOTLIGHT

Following a trail *of any sort requires good balance and coordination. Changing the shape of the path or the distance between the squares, or asking your toddler to jump on and off the path, further challenges that balancing act. Calling out "red," "blue," and "green" as he steps on those colors also helps him expand his vocabulary.*

✔	**Balance**
✔	**Coordination**
✔	**Eye-Foot Coordination**
✔	**Gross Motor Skills**

IF YOUR CHILD ENJOYS THIS ACTIVITY, also try Balancing Act, page 226.

241

BATH TIME FOR BABY

LESSONS IN TENDER, LOVING CARE

SKILLSPOTLIGHT

Two-year-olds are old enough to play "pretend" and to want some measure of control over their world. This activity lets your child be the parent to her "baby" and also allows her to be the little boss – a great way to practice her social skills and exercise her imagination. Learning to hold a soapy doll and wash its tiny body parts also promotes the development of fine motor skills.

Body Awareness	✔
Fine Motor Skills	✔
Imagination	✔
Role-Playing	✔
Social Skills	✔

YOUR LITTLE ONE may already be playing "Mommy" or "Daddy" with her dolls and stuffed animals by rocking them, feeding them, and putting them to bed (see Doll Talk, page 258). She'll love giving her baby dolls baths, too; it's a chance for her to be the caretaker at bath time, to learn about keeping the body clean, and to shower her little friends with love.

• Set up a doll's bathtub by filling a basin – or a baby bathtub if you still have one – with warm, soapy water. Provide towels, washcloths, soap, and bath toys to make it even more realistic.

• Encourage your toddler to test the water's temperature ("Is it too hot for your doll? Is it too cold?") and to be gentle while washing the doll.

• Point out many of the doll's body parts ("That's her nose! And those are her toes!"). This gives your toddler more practice in labeling her own body parts, a favorite activity at this age.

• Pretend the doll is dirty and encourage her to clean behind the doll's ears, between the toes, and in all the other areas that need washing.

• When the doll is clean, let your toddler dry it with a towel. Then remind her to clean one more thing: her dolly's teeth!

◀ *IF YOUR CHILD ENJOYS THIS ACTIVITY, also try Point Out the Parts, page 204.*

24 MONTHS
2
AND UP

SCRUB-A-DUB-DUB, it's dolly in the tub! Your two-year-old will love being in charge of her baby's sudsy sponge bath.

RESEARCH REPORT

A few short months ago, *your toddler wasn't able to engage in this type of imaginative play. Kurt Fischer, a Harvard cognitive neuroscientist and educator, has tracked the cranial growth, brainwave activity, and density of neural connections in children to show that the brain is subject to a series of growth spurts at certain predictable interludes. One such spurt occurs between eighteen and twenty-four months, he says, endowing a child with a capacity for symbolic representation. In other words, for the first time, your child can make the mental leap that an inanimate object (such as her doll) is a "baby" in need of a good washing.*

243

CARE FOR THE ANIMALS

LEARNING TO NURTURE OTHER CREATURES

SKILLSPOTLIGHT

This game of pretend *teaches your child empathy and lets her practice nurturing others. It also helps enhance her awareness of the animal world: birds have wings, tigers have paws, and elephants have trunks. Talking to your child about the ways animals get sick ("The horse ate too much sugar and got a tummy ache") expands her knowledge of them.*

Concept Development	✔
Creative Expression	✔
Fine Motor Skills	✔
Imagination	✔
Role-Playing	✔

SHE LOVES HER ANIMALS (real and stuffed) and she's keen on bandages and the notions of "boo-boo" and "sick." That means she's more than ready to open up a veterinary practice in her own home. It's all pretend, of course, but she'll enjoy learning how to care for her little friends.

• Help your toddler gather her favorite stuffed and plastic animals for this activity. (Make sure the toys are more than 1¾ inches [4.5 cm] in diameter so they won't pose a choking hazard.)

• Provide small boxes or berry baskets for her to use as cages or carriers. She can use napkins or small scarves as blankets.

• Talk to her about the ways in which animals get hurt: how they cut their paws, get bugs in their ears, break their wings, or get stomachaches.

• Help her care for her sick animals by washing and bandaging their wounds, wrapping their broken limbs with gauze, and giving them a clean, quiet place to sleep (plus lots of pats and kind words). A toy doctor's kit will provide helpful instruments for conducting a thorough exam and treatment of her ailing friends, too.

"Is the pony hurt?"

HELPING HER PLAY VET is a natural way to nurture her knowledge of all living things.

245

THE MANY FORMS OF PLAY

WHILE THIS BOOK emphasizes the playful interactions between a parent and child, it's also important to understand how a toddler will play with peers.

One-year-olds are primarily involved in solitary play, busy as they are exploring a world that is totally new to them. They are curious about other children, however, and often will imitate their actions or the noises they make. As they get a little older, toddlers begin engaging in parallel play — that is, two or more youngsters playing with similar toys or activities side by side but without much interaction, such as building block towers individually. Around age two, as child psychologist Penelope Leach notes in *Your Baby and Child,* "Toddlers increasingly need the companionship of other children." Most adore taking part in play groups, but their ability to share toys or to indulge in mannerly back-and-forth exchanges is still a little precarious. As they approach their third birthday, true cooperative play begins to emerge — two toddlers will build a single block tower together, for example — although there are still likely to be standoffs over treasured playthings or the attention of beloved adults.

These early play encounters plant the seeds for acquiring important attributes such as empathy, self-control, sharing, fairness, and self-esteem, and they help cultivate much-needed tools for dealing with different social situations. As Dr. Benjamin Spock explained in *Baby and Child Care,* "In play, children . . . learn how to get along with other children and adults of different personalities, how to enjoy give-and-take, how to solve conflicts." These are valuable lessons indeed, and ones that parents can foster by providing plenty of opportunities for play with other children. ∎

MAGIC CUPS

A CHALLENGING MEMORY GAME

THIS TODDLER ACTIVITY is a step up from peekaboo, but operates on the same principle. First it's here, then it's gone, then it's back again – but only if your toddler remembers where it was! To start the game, hide a small toy under one of three cups while your child is watching. Then move the cups around and ask her to guess which one conceals the toy.

• If you've seen street entertainers play this game, you know it can be confusing, even for adults. So don't move the cups too quickly or else she won't be able to keep track of her toy.

SKILLSPOTLIGHT

When your toddler *was a baby, you could cover up a toy and she would forget it ever existed. Now she understands that the covered object is still there – this is called object permanence – and she's delighted to find it. By asking her to concentrate on one cup as it moves, you encourage her to re-call the toy and you help sharpen her visual memory.*

| ✔ | **Problem Solving** |
| ✔ | **Visual Memory** |

WHICH CUP HIDES THE YELLOW ducky? She'll love trying to keep tabs – especially if you applaud her when she's right.

247

BEEP, BEEP

PLAYING WITH TRUCKS AND CARS

SKILLSPOTLIGHT

Playing with toy cars *is a great way for your toddler to exercise her imagination, and it gives her a chance to imitate a mundane part of your adult world: driving the car. (Don't worry; it's interesting to her!) It also lets her develop the fine motor skills of pushing and pulling and teaches her to discern noises in her everyday world.*

Creative Expression	✔
Fine Motor Skills	✔
Imagination	✔
Language Development	✔

MOST TWO-YEAR-OLDS are fascinated with all things vehicular, ranging from their own strollers to the cars, trucks, and buses on the street to the choo-choo trains they see in picture books. They're especially excited by watching trains and cars enter tunnels and cross bridges. Enhance their wonder (and let them feel like they're finally behind the wheel of one of these grown-up contraptions) by giving them a chance to play with toy trucks, cars, and tunnels.

• Choose a large, colorful toy vehicle, rather than a miniature one, so she can control it more easily.

• Show her how to push the truck along the floor. Teach her all of the noises it makes, including the "beep, beep" of the horn, the "scre-e-e-ch" of the tires, and the "vrooom" of the engine. Point out those same sounds to her when you're driving in a real automobile.

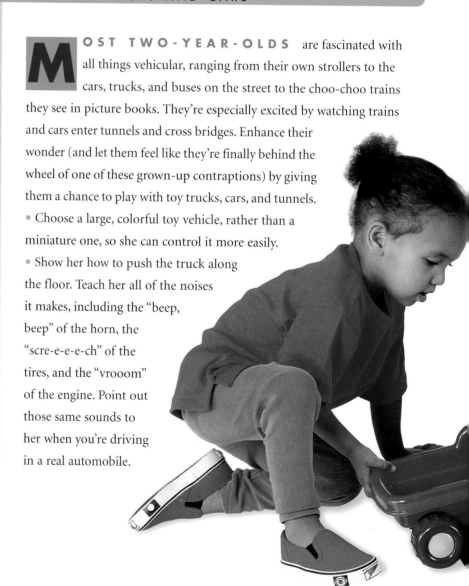

• Cut holes in both ends of a big cardboard box to make a tunnel and show her how to push the truck through it. Talk about the different parts of the truck (steering wheel, tires) and explain why she might need to "turn on" the headlights when she drives into the dark tunnel. Also see if she can guess which part of the truck will come out of the tunnel first — the front or the back.

STEER HER ENERGY into a little creative car play, and watch those motor skills grow.

RESEARCH REPORT

A toddler's *apparently boundless enthusiasm for play reflects the fact that she is in a unique and wondrous period of development. A child's brain at age two years consumes twice as much metabolic energy as an adult's, and it possesses twice as many synapses (the connections between nerve cells that convey the electrical impulses needed for all the body's functions, including cognition). "Children are biologically primed for learning during this time,"* state neurologist Ann Barnet and her co-author and husband, Richard, in their book The Youngest Minds. *This golden window of opportunity lasts only until age ten or so, when the brain starts to lose the synaptic connections that haven't yet been put to use.*

249

DRIVE THE FIRE TRUCK

A FAVORITE MOVEMENT SONG

 to the *tune* of **"Ten Little Indians"**

Hurry, hurry,
drive the fire truck,
make driving motions
hurry, hurry,
drive the fire truck,
hurry, hurry,
drive the fire truck,
ding, ding, ding, ding, ding!
swing hand as if ringing a bell

Hurry, hurry,
climb the ladder,
pretend to climb a ladder
hurry, hurry,
climb the ladder,
hurry, hurry,
climb the ladder,
ding, ding, ding, ding, ding!

Hurry, hurry,
squirt the water,
make squirting motions
hurry, hurry,
squirt the water,
hurry, hurry,
squirt the water,
ding, ding, ding, ding, ding!

Language Development	✔
Role-Playing	✔

RING THE BELL! Sound the alarm! This fast-paced song lets your truck-loving tyke pretend to drive the biggest, brightest rig around – a fire truck – while letting him play one of the most exciting roles in town. Face your child while you teach him the hand gestures, or have him stand with his back to you and help him do them himself. If he is ready to act out the role of a firefighter, find a heavy-duty cardboard box, paint it bright red, and push him around in it as you sing "Hurry, Hurry, Drive the Fire Truck" and he makes the motions.

YOUR LITTLE FIRE CHIEF will think this is the hottest game of all when he realizes he gets to drive the truck and put out the imaginary fire with his pretend hose.

PURSE TREASURES

EXPLORING GOODIES IN THE BAG

GRANTED, A TODDLER'S boundless curiosity about the treasures in your purse or briefcase is adorable. But it can lead to chaos (like lost credit cards) and even danger (opened pillboxes and pointy pencils). Safely encourage her explorations by giving her a purse of her very own. Fill it with harmless objects such as those she might find in your bag: a comb, keys, mirror, notepad — even a wallet. Encourage her to find things without looking ("Can you feel the keys in there?"), or ask her to name each item as she pulls it out.

IT LOOKS LIKE she's just playing grown-up. But her very own bag – filled with safe items from a parent's briefcase – lets her explore different objects and learn about their uses.

SKILLSPOTLIGHT

You can enrich *your child's understanding of all the items in her purse by explaining the use of each object as she pulls it out ("I'm glad you found the car keys. Now we can drive to the grocery store." Or, "Would you like to comb your hair with that?"). Frequently changing the objects in the purse further challenges your child's identifying skills.*

✓	**Concept Development**
✓	**Language Development**
✓	**Listening Skills**
✓	**Tactile Discrimination**

TOUCH AND TELL

WHAT'S IN THE PILLOWCASE?

SKILLSPOTLIGHT

Learning to describe *the objects in his world helps your child feel some measure of control over them. It also helps him develop his language skills. And adding a tactile component to his developing visual memory helps him understand objects in a three-dimensional way.*

Concept Development	✔
Language Development	✔
Listening Skills	✔
Problem Solving	✔
Tactile Discrimination	✔

YOUR TODDLER is getting into just about everything now, mostly because he's compelled to explore how everything feels, tastes, sounds, looks, and moves. Help him investigate and identify the sensations of different shapes and textures with this variation of the classic show-and-tell game.

• Place a familiar object such as his toy truck, ball, doll, or favorite spoon or cup inside a pillowcase or canvas bag.

• Ask your child to reach into the pillowcase (no peeking!) and feel the object. Then ask him to guess what it is. (He may need to guess more than once.) If he doesn't guess the right answer, tell him what it is before he grows too frustrated.

• Pull out the object and talk to him about its tactile characteristics. Introduce the concepts of hard and soft, fuzzy and smooth.

• Put another toy inside and repeat the exercise. Encourage him to use the words you've introduced as he's guessing what the toy is.

• To vary the game, let him hide a toy in the pillowcase so you can play detective. Also try putting an object inside and asking your young sleuth to guess what it is by feeling it from *outside* the pillowcase.

IF YOUR CHILD ENJOYS THIS ACTIVITY, also try Mystery Sounds, page 257.

24 MONTHS
2
AND UP

"Look! It's my cup!"

HE'LL GET A FEEL for textures and learn to name those sensations in this hands-on guessing game.

253

TURN HER LOOSE with some tools and colorful clay, and watch her creativity take shape.

RESEARCHREPORT

Squishing and shaping
modeling clay does more than encourage the budding artist in your child. By allowing her to handle these and other tactile delights, you're helping her develop "knowledge of how the world works and proficiency at using different materials," states Esther Thelen, a psychologist at Indiana University in Bloomington. Educational psychologist Jane Healy is another believer in the benefits of clay, sand, finger paint, and mud, which she says help refine a child's tactile ability. She also offers this advice to fastidious parents: "If you tend to be fanatic about cleanliness, close your eyes and imagine little [neural] dendrites branching inside that muddy head."

254

PLAY WITH CLAY

MAKING SHAPES AND SCULPTURES

YOU MAY HAVE FOND MEMORIES of molding clay into silly shapes, and now your two-year-old is ready to dive into the colorful stuff. Purchase non-toxic modeling clay in any toy store or make a few colorful batches yourself (see the recipe for clay at right). Provide ample working space and a few safe tools, such as a rolling pin, a potato masher, and cookie cutters. Then let the sculpting begin.

• Most young children prefer to experiment with mushing the clay into abstract shapes. Guide her in manipulating the clay by rolling it into a ball and letting her smash it. Or make a long roll that she can tear into pieces and press back together.

• Show your child how simple shapes such as circles, squares, and triangles fit together to make recognizable objects like faces, hats, or trees.

• To store the clay, gather several airtight containers and mark each lid with the same color as the clay it contains. When she's done playing with the clay, ask her to put it in its appropriate container.

MAKING YOUR OWN

Mix 1 cup flour, 1 cup salt, 1 tablespoon cream of tartar, 1 cup water, and 1 tablespoon vegetable oil. Simmer in a pot until clay begins to pull away from the pot's sides. When cool, add 5 drops of food coloring, and knead until smooth.

SKILLSPOTLIGHT

Playing with modeling clay
allows your child to experience shapes and textures in three dimensions. In addition, manipulating the clay stimulates the senses and builds fine motor skills. Help increase your child's vocabulary by teaching her the words for colors, shapes, and textures.

✔	**Cause & Effect**
✔	**Creative Expression**
✔	**Fine Motor Skills**
✔	**Language Development**
✔	**Sensory Exploration**

◀ *IF YOUR CHILD ENJOYS THIS ACTIVITY, also try Sand Skills, page 192.*

255

IF THE SHOE FITS

SORTING SHOES OF SEVERAL SIZES

SKILLSPOTLIGHT

This easy-to-assemble *project allows toddlers to practice their early sorting skills and make discoveries about size and materials. As you talk together, your toddler's use of language expands; when you ask him to guess or make assumptions about the different shoes and their uses, you encourage the development of his problem-solving abilities.*

| **Classifying Skills** | ✔ |
| **Language Development** | ✔ |

IF YOUR CHILD ENJOYS THIS ACTIVITY, *also try Car Capers, page 280.* ▶

MANY CLASSIFYING ACTIVITIES are too frustrating for younger toddlers, but by age two to two-and-a-half, most children are eager to perform a fairly simple sorting task — especially if it involves playing with Mommy's or Daddy's shoes. Put two or three pairs of shoes on a table, separating each shoe from its mate. Choose shoes of distinct sizes and types, such as adult boots, baby shoes, and your fuzzy slippers. Ask your child which shoes match. As he searches for the mate, talk about the types of shoes, whom they fit, and what they're used for. Some toddlers find it easier to sort if they have shoe boxes to put the pairs into.

WHICH SHOES BELONG together? Toddlers can try to successfully combine pairs of family footwear in a challenging game of mix-and-match.

256

MYSTERY SOUNDS

FINDING THE HIDDEN NOISE

WHAT'S THAT SOUND? Where is it coming from? Those are the questions to pose to young detectives in this game of auditory hide-and-seek. Use a long-playing musical toy or other noisemaking item (such as a kitchen timer, clock, or metronome) and hide it on a low shelf or table – or behind a cupboard door. Search together with your child to locate the source of the sound and retrieve the object. As you hunt, ask your toddler to try to guess what toy or object is making the mysterious sound.

USING HER EARS to find the source of a sound may become a young sleuth's favorite guessing game.

SKILLSPOTLIGHT

Young children love *guessing games, and this one helps fine-tune auditory skills. Locating an object by listening to a sound teaches your toddler to find an answer through the process of elimination – and it reinforces the notion that a thoughtful guess is part of the learning process.*

✔ **Listening Skills**

✔ **Problem Solving**

IF YOUR CHILD ENJOYS THIS ACTIVITY, also try Mighty Megaphones, page 283.

257

DOLL TALK

LEARNING TO NURTURE

SKILLSPOTLIGHT

Toddlers learn *to be kind to others – whether they are animals or people – often by watching their parents' behavior. Participating in your child's doll (or animal) play gives you the opportunity to model appropriate words and gestures. It also gives her a chance to feel confident about her emerging feelings of gentleness and love.*

Creative Expression	✔
Fine Motor Skills	✔
Imagination	✔
Listening Skills	✔
Social Skills	✔

SEEING A TODDLER'S TENDERNESS toward the dolls, teddies, and other cuddlies in her world is truly touching. Her enthusiasm, however, may sometimes make her a bit too rough — especially with animals or other children. You can help refine her nurturing abilities by interacting with your child as she plays with her pretend friends.

• Give your child a favorite doll or stuffed animal to hold. Suggest that she gently brush the doll's hair or rock it in her arms. Or help her learn to pat animals by showing her how on a plush toy.

• Tell her that the doll or teddy bear is cold, and ask her to comfort it by putting shoes and socks and warm clothes on the doll (she may need help with snaps and buttons) or by covering a plush toy with a blanket.

• Then suggest that she feed her doll or pet because it hasn't eaten all day and must be quite hungry. She can offer it pretend food, or give her a spoon and a small dish of cereal or raisins, which are easy to clean up.

• Join your child in singing a favorite lullaby to her charge while helping her rock it to sleep, then ask her to gently tuck it into bed.

IF YOUR CHILD ENJOYS THIS ACTIVITY, also try Bath Time for Baby, page 242.

RESEARCH REPORT

While many adults *still struggle with the finer points of grammar, we might be humbled to learn that 90 percent of the sentences spoken by the average three-year-old are grammatically correct. The mistakes they make usually result from an overly zealous application of the rules. For example, in English we usually indicate plurals by adding an "s" or "es" to the end of a noun – rivers, churches – and we use the suffix "ed" to convey the past tense of verbs – patted, changed, kissed. So why do we laugh at a toddler who says, "I want three mouses" or "You gave me a doll"? Hey, she's just following the rules!*

WHEN DADDY SHOWS his daughter how to care for her doll, he provides an important lesson in nurturing others.

COLOR CLUSTERS

A SORTING, SPINNING, AND COUNTING ACTIVITY

SKILLSPOTLIGHT

This elementary abacus *enhances your toddler's ability to categorize objects by helping him identify different colors and sizes. It also provides a great opportunity to introduce your child to comparison words, such as big, bigger, and biggest.*

COLORFUL, REVOLVING BALLS on a rope are sure to catch toddlers' eyes, as they love both bright colors and spinning motions. But besides being fun, this activity can teach your little one some pretty big concepts. To start, thread a thin rope through a group of colored balls with holes (available at many toy stores) and tie the rope firmly between two chairs. Show your toddler how to spin the balls and slide them from one end of the rope to the other. Then ask him to spin only a particular color or only the large balls.

Classifying Skills	✔
Concept Development	✔
Coordination	✔
Language Development	✔

MAKING THE BRIGHT BALLS spin quickly is fun, but so is learning to identify blue and red, large and small, and more and less.

260

30 MONTHS
2½
AND UP

WATER TARGETS

MAKING A SPLASH LANDING

WATER, BALLS, THROWING, SPLASHING – the elements in this activity may get you and your toddler a bit wet, but she'll enjoy it so much you won't mind. Find two or three big plastic bowls or pots and fill them halfway with water. Gather an assortment of small balls, preferably ones that float (plastic or tennis balls work well). Ask your child to throw the balls into the water targets. Count how many balls she can land inside each bowl and be sure to applaud every attempt, even when she misses. As she gets better at this activity, increase the challenge by having her stand farther away from the bowls.

YOUR LITTLE PITCHER makes a big splash when she gets the ball in – and she fine-tunes her coordination skills as she aims for her water targets.

SKILLSPOTLIGHT

This water game *helps build your toddler's eye-hand coordination and gross motor skills. The activity is also a fun way to introduce your toddler to counting ("That's one in, two in. Look! Three balls in the water!").*

✔ **Coordination**

✔ **Counting Concepts**

✔ **Eye-Hand Coordination**

✔ **Gross Motor Skills**

IF YOUR CHILD ENJOYS THIS ACTIVITY, also try Up It Goes!, page 266. ▶

261

"I found Teddy!"

A TREASURE HUNT becomes even more exciting – and challenging – for your child when she has a flashlight to use in the dark.

262

FLASHLIGHT FUN

30 MONTHS
2½
AND UP

FINDING HIDDEN TOYS IN THE DARK

WIELDING A FLASHLIGHT sparks wonder in most toddlers: the tool gives them control over the dark and changes the look of everything around them.

- Start this activity in the evening by hiding one of your child's favorite items, such as a doll, a book, or her beloved teddy bear. Limit the hunting area to one or two rooms so it won't be too difficult for her to find the hidden treasure.

- Tell your toddler what to look for, turn off (or just dim) the lights, and hand her a lightweight flashlight. (You may have to show her how to use it at first.) Be sure to equip yourself with a flashlight too, so you can join in the fun.

- Keep the game lively and silly by providing her with several clues: "You're getting warmer, warmer, warmer! Oops! Now you're cooling down." If she starts to get a little frustrated, use the beam of your own flashlight to help guide her to the hiding place.

- This is an ideal activity for a toddler to play with an older sibling or a group of kids, because you can hide several objects at one time – some in harder places than others – and it's a great spectacle to watch the children waving their bright beams of light at one another.

IF YOUR CHILD ENJOYS THIS ACTIVITY, also try Purse Treasures, page 251.

SKILLSPOTLIGHT

Searching for an object *presents a problem that your child has to concentrate on in order to solve. The first step for her, of course, is to listen to your description of the hidden object, which involves comprehension skills. Then she has to think about places that aren't immediately visible to her – a type of abstract thinking that is a big step for a young child. This nighttime game may also allay fears and negative feelings that children often have about darkness.*

✔	**Listening Skills**
✔	**Problem Solving**
✔	**Social Skills**
✔	**Visual Memory**

NATURE VS. NURTURE

DO WE COME into this world imprinted with immutable abilities, foibles, and personality traits? Or are we born blank slates, waiting for the environment to etch its effect on our psyches? For many scientists, the new influx of brain research has settled the age-old question of nature versus nurture once and for all. The verdict? It's a draw.

For decades, behavioral studies have suggested that some traits, such as aggressiveness, shyness, and a willingness to take risks, have a genetic origin. But just when Mother Nature seemed to be the winner in the ancient debate, neurologists demonstrated how unfinished the human brain is at birth and how environmental factors exert powerful influences on a person's disposition — even altering the shape of the brain in some cases. Scientists in the 1990s have reconciled these two competing forces by concluding that while people are indeed born with certain tendencies and abilities, the degree to which those traits are manifested depends a great deal on what people are exposed to, especially during early childhood. As neurologist Ann Barnet states in her book *The Youngest Minds,* "Current estimates made by behavioral geneticists for the relative influence of heritable factors and environment are about 50-50."

This split has important implications for parents. For one thing, it means that if a child is innately inclined to some particular behavior, parents can work with her to overcome that tendency — helping her become more outgoing if she's shy, for example, or instilling a little impulse control if she's inclined to take too many risks. Conversely, it also suggests that even if a child is born with certain gifts, such as outstanding musical or artistic ability, those talents might never be realized if there's no opportunity for them to flourish. ■

HEY MR. JUMPING JACK

30 MONTHS AND UP 2½

WIGGLE AND SHAKE TO A BEAT

GET YOUR LITTLE ONE giggling and wiggling to this upbeat chant that encourages rhythm and movement. Hold your child on your lap, facing you, and then tap out a rhythm with your feet as you say the words. When Mr. Jumping Jack jumps high, lift your toddler up high; when he jumps low, give him just a little lift. For the second verse, wiggle your child gently as you lift him high and low (hard shaking is dangerous). Add your own verses and movements – clapping, flapping, and waving, for example. And when your toddler is steady on his feet, let him jump and wiggle on his own as you chant and clap.

SECURE in Mommy's arms, your toddler will laugh out loud as he soars up and down to the words of this cheery chant.

Hey Mr. Jumping Jack,
a funny old man,
he jumps and he jumps
whenever he can.
He jumps way up high,
he jumps way down low,
and he jumps and he jumps
wherever he goes.

Come on and jump!

Hey Mr. Jumping Jack,
a funny old man,
he wiggles and he wiggles
whenever he can.
He wiggles way up high,
he wiggles way down low,
and he wiggles and he wiggles
wherever he goes.

Come on and wiggle!

✓ **Listening Skills**
✓ **Rhythm Exploration**

IF YOUR CHILD ENJOYS THIS ACTIVITY, also try Teddy Bear Tunes, page 270. ▶

UP IT GOES!

A BALL-AND-PARACHUTE GAME

SKILLSPOTLIGHT

This game challenges *your toddler's coordination and visual acuity. To toss the ball straight up, she has to try to raise the blanket in sync with you. To catch it squarely on the blanket, she needs to keep her eye on the ball as it comes back down. This activity takes planning and some sense of cooperation with her partner – and she may need to practice it several times before she catches on.*

Cause & Effect	✔
Eye-Foot Coordination	✔
Eye-Hand Coordination	✔

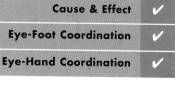

◄ IF YOUR CHILD ENJOYS THIS ACTIVITY, *also try Beach-Ball Catch, page 225.*

SUMMER OR WINTER, indoors or out, a beach ball – or another very lightweight ball – makes for all kinds of merriment when there's a toddler around. To play this game, you and your child hold opposite ends of a blanket or parachute. Place a beach ball in the center and toss it up in the air, catching it in the parachute as it comes down again. Start with gentle tosses so the ball doesn't go too high. As your toddler's coordination improves, bounce the ball higher and higher.

SHE FOLLOWS the bouncing ball in this delightful game that exercises her ability to coordinate muscle movements with motion.

PAPER PUZZLE

FITTING THE BIG PIECES TOGETHER

IF YOUR CHILD is already happily playing with wooden puzzles and shape sorters, it might be a prime time to enhance his ability to understand and organize shapes spatially by creating an elementary puzzle for him. Find an engaging, colorful picture of something your toddler might like – an animal, a truck, a baby, or a favorite food, for instance. (Magazines are rich sources for large photographs.) Then glue the image onto a letter-size piece of paper or cardboard. Cut the picture into four large sections. Now help him rearrange the pieces to put the picture back together again. When he's figured that out, you can make the puzzle more difficult by cutting it into smaller pieces.

PUTTING TWO AND TWO together to make a butterfly is just the kind of puzzle your toddler is now ready to tackle.

SKILL SPOTLIGHT

This activity allows *your toddler to exercise his understanding of spatial relations. It also lets him create – and recreate – a picture that he likes (a test of his visual memory skills), which will give him the confidence to eventually try more difficult puzzles.*

✔	**Concept Development**
✔	**Problem Solving**
✔	**Size & Shape Discrimination**
✔	**Visual Discrimination**
✔	**Visual Memory**

267

COMMON SCENTS

AN ODYSSEY OF ODORS

SKILLSPOTLIGHT

Here's an activity *that lets your child further explore the many aspects of her sensory world. Bringing the realm of scents to her attention helps her become more aware of the hundreds of different odors – pleasant and pungent – around us. Teaching her the words for different smells, and the objects from which they emanate, also expands her vocabulary.*

Language Development	✔
Problem Solving	✔
Sensory Exploration	✔
Visual Memory	✔

SHE SMILES WHEN EATING a cookie and purses her little lips at the sight of broccoli, so you know she has a discriminating palate. But how's her sense of smell? Help her learn to match aroma to food with this simple sniffing game.

• Gather several strongly scented foods that your child already knows, such as chocolate-chip cookies, oranges, and onions.

• Blindfold her with a handkerchief or scarf (or just cover her eyes with your hand). Then ask her to take a big sniff (no peeking!) and guess what the smells are. After she guesses, let her taste the food to better match different smells with different tastes.

• As she masters this activity, choose foods with more subtle aromas. For example, see if she can distinguish between a peach and an apple, a cookie and a cake, or a lemon and an orange.

• You can do this with outside smells, too. Test her olfactory memory on flowers, pine needles, damp dirt, and common herbs.

• Or ask your toddler to identify smells she might encounter in the neighborhood, such as fresh bread in a bakery, barbecued chicken in a restaurant, or summer fruits at a sidewalk stand.

IF YOUR CHILD ENJOYS THIS ACTIVITY, also try Touch and Tell, page 252.

"What are you smelling now?"

PHEW! The pungent smell of raw onion is easy to recognize, but how about those orange slices?

TEDDY BEAR TUNES

TODDLERS LOVE teddy bears — and the rhythm and repetition of these teddy tunes give them a timeless appeal. With your child on your knee, bounce her gently to the beat of these songs while encouraging her to sing along — or join her (and her plush toys) in acting out the appropriate gestures.

THE BEAR

to the tune of **"For He's a Jolly Good Fellow"**

The bear went over the mountain,
the bear went over the mountain,
the bear went over the mountain,
to see what she could see.

To see what she could see,
To see what she could see.

The bear went over the mountain,
the bear went over the mountain,
the bear went over the mountain,
to see what she could see.

TEDDY BEAR, TEDDY BEAR

Teddy bear, teddy bear, turn around.
*turn around in circles with your child
as you teach her this chant*

**Teddy bear, teddy bear,
touch the ground.**
touch the floor

**Teddy bear, teddy bear,
show your shoe.**
bring one foot forward

**Teddy bear, teddy bear,
crawl right through.**
let your child crawl between your legs

MARCHING BEARS

 to the tune of "The Saints Go Marching In"

**Oh when the bears
go marching in,
oh when the bears go marching in,
oh, how I want to be a big teddy,
when the bears go marching in.**
march in place with your child

**Oh when the bears
go jumping in,
oh when the bears go jumping in,
oh, how I want to be a big teddy,
when the bears go jumping in.**
jump up and down

**Oh when the bears
go wiggling in . . .**
wiggle your body

**Oh when the bears
go tiptoeing in . . .**
tiptoe around the room

**Oh when the bears
go hopping in . . .**
hop up and down

BEARS ARE SLEEPING

 to the tune of "Frère Jacques"

**Bears are sleeping,
bears are sleeping,
in their caves, in their caves.
Waiting for the springtime,
waiting for the springtime.
Shh! Shh! Shh!
Shh! Shh! Shh!**

DADDY'S KNEE is the perfect place for a duet of teddy bear songs that will help your young cub expand her language and listening skills.

271

ON TARGET!

LANDING ON THE MARK

The act of jumping *works muscles on both sides of the body, thereby increasing bilateral coordination. This provides a good counterpoint to activities, such as rolling a ball, that work only one side of the body. Jumping also improves eye-foot coordination and balance in an older toddler: she needs to put her feet where she's looking and then she has to try to stay upright after landing.*

Balance	✔
Eye-Foot Coordination	✔
Gross Motor Skills	✔
Spatial Awareness	✔

JUMPING IS A BIG ACCOMPLISHMENT for toddlers, one that takes coordination, strength, and a dash of courage. It's also a skill that thrills: just observe the joy on your puddle jumper's face after leaping into a big pool of rainwater. You can help improve her form and aim and boost her confidence by setting up jumping target practice using a stable stool, block, or another safe launching pad that won't slide out from beneath her.

• Use a large piece of construction paper or a colored paper plate as a target, and adhere it to the ground with strong packaging tape so it won't slip when she lands. Encourage your child to jump directly onto the target — this will likely take some practice. Applaud every attempt.

• As your toddler's abilities increase, make the target smaller. Or ask her to jump from a greater (though still safe) height.

• Some children may be nervous about bounding into space this way. Soothe her fears by showing her how to jump — or hold her hand as she makes the leap. Once she becomes confident in her jumping abilities, she'll want to aim for the target again and again.

IF YOUR CHILD ENJOYS THIS ACTIVITY, also try Turn Around, page 277. ▶

READY? SET. GO! This aerial joyride is a jumping-off point for building strong muscles and eye-foot coordination.

RESEARCH REPORT

Enriching experiences *such as assembling a collage provide children with creative stimulation that is vital to their development. Researchers at Baylor College of Medicine in Houston, Texas, found that children deprived of playthings and playmates (as well as nurturing caregivers) have brains 20 to 30 percent smaller than normal. To provide the proper stimulation, parents needn't stock up on all sorts of techno-gadgets and expensive toys; an extensive study conducted at the University of Alabama found that the basics, such as art supplies, blocks, and puzzles, were still the best at promoting cognitive and physical development.*

274

COLORFUL COLLAGES

COLLECTING INTRIGUING IMAGES

EVEN AT THIS EARLY AGE, your child has distinct likes and dislikes. He may be fascinated by music, for instance, or animals, or occupations such as gardening and cooking. Encourage him to enjoy his natural interests by helping him create a fun collage made from related pictures.

• Collect colorful pictures of his current passion from magazines, newspapers, or even junk mail, and place them in a big basket or bowl.

• Invite your toddler to look through them and talk about the pictures as he picks them up. Ask him to name the objects he sees (for example, a violin, a whale, a flower, a blueberry muffin).

• Ask him to pick out his favorite pictures. Place them on a large sheet of heavyweight paper, such as construction paper.

• Using children's (nontoxic) glue, show him how to put glue onto the back of a picture, then press it down onto the paper to make a collage.

• Once you both have completed the collage, hang it someplace visible, such as in his bedroom, on the refrigerator, or even in the front hallway. Children's art should be seen – not hidden!

SKILL SPOTLIGHT

Letting your child *select his own pictures for a collage gives him a chance to practice expressing his preferences. Encouraging him to discuss the images is a way to help build his vocabulary. And teaching him to handle glue and sticky pieces of paper aids him in developing his fine motor skills.*

✔ **Creative Expression**

✔ **Fine Motor Skills**

✔ **Language Development**

✔ **Visual Discrimination**

"I LIKE DOLPHINS because they live in the ocean." Learn more about your child while creating a work of art that reflects his personality and preferences.

IF YOUR CHILD ENJOYS THIS ACTIVITY, also try Paper Puzzle, page 267.

BEAUTIFUL BOX

DECORATING A TOY CHEST

SKILLSPOTLIGHT

This project nurtures *a toddler's creative spirit while encouraging her to express herself on something other than flat paper. By combining drawing, painting, coloring, and collage, it introduces her to several different artistic media. This activity also polishes fine motor skills and can help develop communication skills, especially if parents engage their children in a discussion as they're decorating the box together.*

Creative Expression	✔
Fine Motor Skills	✔
Social Skills	✔

TAKE YOUR TODDLER'S natural (albeit elementary) artistic abilities to a new dimension by helping her decorate a box for her toy treasures. Use a plain or colored cardboard box (or cover a printed box with white paper). Give your child non-permanent markers and crayons for drawing lines and circles on the box; help her glue glitter, ribbons, or paper cutouts on it as well. You can start with a theme (such as the sea) and encourage her to elaborate on that topic with stickers of waves, fish, boats, and beach balls. When she's done, write her name on her special box.

TURN HER LOOSE with crayons and stickers, and watch her create a treasure chest of her own.

IF YOUR CHILD ENJOYS THIS ACTIVITY, also try Play With Clay, page 254.

276

TURN AROUND

30 MONTHS $2\frac{1}{2}$ **AND UP**

A SING-WHILE-YOU-SPIN SONG

THIS MOVE-YOUR-BODY SONG is a fun way to combine singing with some vigorous exercise. Sing "Turn Around" a few times, following the instructions in the lyrics, and exaggerate your actions — for example, leap high in the air when you sing, "Up we go!" Your little jumping bean will love imitating you; at the same time he'll develop better body control and gross motor skills. Acting out the lyrics also improves your child's comprehension of up and down and high and low.

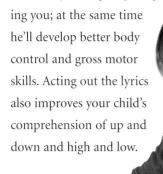

MOVING TO THE MUSIC helps his body confidence grow by leaps and bounds.

to the tune of **"Frère Jacques"**

Perform the actions as indicated by the lyrics; do them slowly until your child understands all the movements.

**Turn around,
turn around,
touch your toes,
touch your toes.**

**Do a little jumping,
do a little jumping.**

Squat real low.

Up we go!

✔	**Balance**
✔	**Coordination**
✔	**Gross Motor Skills**

IF YOUR CHILD ENJOYS THIS ACTIVITY, also try Head to Toes, page 232.

277

MINI MIMES

ACTING OUT A TEA PARTY

SKILLSPOTLIGHT

Toddlers love to assist *adults and to perform all the grown-up tasks they do. These miming games let your child delve into an imaginary world that includes an adult and adult activities – the perfect combination. Cooperating on a joint project – however imaginary – also helps her learn social skills such as sharing, offering, and expressing gratitude.*

Body Awareness	✔
Creative Expression	✔
Creative Movement	✔
Imagination	✔
Social Skills	✔

SHE WANTS TO DO just about everything you do, right? Let her participate in grown-up activities by miming all sorts of fun things along with you.

• Try having a tea party – with no tea set. Act out pouring the tea, passing the plate of cookies, and drinking and eating. Be sure to say "Please," "Thank you," and "Mmm . . . this is delicious!" That helps her to learn good manners, and the conversation brings the party to life.

• Bake a cake together without any pans or ingredients. Crack the pretend eggs, mix in the flour, and pour the batter into a pan. Dust the flour off your hands when you're all done – and then treat yourselves to a big piece of scrumptious cake.

• Other activities to act out include flying an airplane, cleaning up the house, or galloping around on a horse.

"This is delicious tea!"

IT'S JUST PRETEND TEA, but a play tea party fires up her imagination and teaches her to say "Yes, please, I would love some more" and "Thank you very much."

CAR CAPERS

A MATCHING-COLORS GAME

SKILLSPOTLIGHT

Successfully matching colors *helps train a toddler's eye to compare and contrast different objects. It also engages his mind by making him link up two very different items that share one common characteristic (in this case, color). And repeating the names of the colors aloud as he matches the car to the paper helps strengthen his vocabulary.*

Classifying Skills	✔
Concept Development	✔
Problem Solving	✔
Visual Discrimination	✔

IF YOUR CHILD ENJOYS THIS ACTIVITY, *also try Leaf Lineup, page 289.*

MOST TWO-YEAR-OLDS are fascinated by colors and are compelled to identify them. This activity takes advantage of your child's interest in colors while strengthening his ability to recognize them. Find some paper that matches the colors of the cars or trucks and other vehicles in his toy collection. Call out the color of the paper as you lay it on the floor. Park a car of the same color on each piece of paper (red car on red paper, yellow truck on yellow paper, for example). Then mix them up and ask your child to "drive" the vehicles onto their correct, color-coded parking spots.

FINDING THE RIGHT parking place helps him begin to recognize what two different objects have in common.

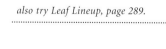

280

FUNNY FACES

TALKING ABOUT FEELINGS

YOUR TODDLER is just beginning to understand the concept of emotions – that he feels happy sometimes and perhaps angry or sad at other times. Wooden spoon puppets can help him identify and express his feelings in appropriate ways. Draw a happy face, a sad face, and a mad face on three wooden spoons. You can also dress them up with construction paper: add "hair," a "mustache," or a bow tie. Have the spoons express their "feelings" to your child or to each other. The happy-face spoon can say, "Oh boy! I'm going to the zoo today!" And the mad face can say, "No! I don't want to wear my coat!" Encourage your child to express his emotions, too.

SKILLSPOTLIGHT

Up until a few months ago, *your child probably had only one way of expressing "difficult" feelings: crying. Now he's getting old enough to say when he's happy, sad, or mad. Spoon puppets can model such conversations for him. Notice how he's getting rather demanding these days? Let the happy-face spoon show him how to politely ask for a glass of water instead of insisting on one.*

✔ **Concept Development**

✔ **Creative Expression**

✔ **Language Development**

✔ **Social Skills**

IT'S OFTEN EASIER for children to express themselves through play – so let your toddler practice talking about feelings with spoon puppets.

281

TODDLER TALK

JUST AS CHILDREN seem to come into this world hard-wired to learn language, parents instinctively do much to promote this vital skill. In countless cultures around the world, for example, they naturally speak to their babies and toddlers in a high-pitched, repetitive, singsong voice that linguists have dubbed "parentese." It is now universally accepted that this melodic, pared-down speech speeds up a child's ability to connect words with the objects they represent and offers the simplified syntax and repetition she needs to learn many of the rules of grammar.

Parents can do several other things to help. As the Research Report on page 183 highlights, the simple act of talking to your child – a lot –even before she is capable of talking back is critical to building her vocabulary. "Tell your baby and toddler everything you can think of," advise Dr. Marian Diamond and Janet Hopson in *Magic Trees of the Mind*. "Bathe your child with spoken language." Having a toddler point to the pictures in a book, echo some of your words, or add sound effects keeps her engaged and helps stretch her attention span.

Introducing new words in a real-life, emotional context also is important – a child picks up the meaning of "later" and "now" much more quickly when the words are linked to the time that she's going to get a favorite snack or go to the park. Feeding her boundless interest in knowing the names of everything she sees in the house, passes in the car, or spots in the local market is key to fulfilling her labeling instinct, which is going full throttle as she approaches her second birthday. Finally, keep in mind the benefits of hands-on parenting: cuddling a child as you talk or read together adds a dimension of loving, physical contact that also seems to hasten language acquisition. ■

MIGHTY MEGAPHONES

30 MONTHS
2½
AND UP

FUN WITH BOOMING VOICES

SHE'S SPEAKING quite well now, and her vocalizations often range from a murmur (when she's "reading" to her teddy bear) to a shriek (when it's time to leave the playground). You can expand her verbal and auditory skills even further with a paper megaphone. Just roll up a big sheet of thick paper and show her how talking into the small end of the cone can change the tone, direction, and volume of her voice. Take turns talking loudly and softly with the megaphone, or use it for amplifying songs and silly sounds.

NOW HEAR THIS: She'll love expanding her vocal range with this improvised amplifier.

SKILLSPOTLIGHT

Children naturally explore *their senses during play, but this activity encourages a focused exploration of listening and making sounds. Toddlers are also natural performers (hence the physical frenzy that often greets guests). Improvising with this megaphone helps turn up the volume on their creativity.*

✔	**Cause & Effect**
✔	**Creative Expression**
✔	**Listening Skills**
✔	**Sensory Exploration**

283

RIBBON RINGS

FANCY DANCING WITH FLYING STREAMERS

SKILL SPOTLIGHT

When you add *ribbon rings to a toddler's dance session, she'll become more aware of how she's moving her arms and body to make the ribbons float in different ways. This helps her develop gross motor skills and coordination. The rings also encourage rhythm exploration as well as creativity.*

Body Awareness	✔
Coordination	✔
Creative Movement	✔
Gross Motor Skills	✔
Rhythm Exploration	✔

S **HE ALREADY LOVES** to dance, but adding rings of colorful, floating ribbon will make her spinning and twirling all the more magical — and fun.

● Purchase a pair of ribbon rings (sold at specialty toy stores) or make your own by buying a dozen fabric ribbons or cutting fabric or old sheets into strips that are between 12 and 25 inches (30 to 64 cm) in length. Securely tie one end of each of the ribbons or strips around small embroidery rings or canning rims.

284

• Talk to your child about the different colors of the ribbons and ask her to show you which one is her favorite.

• Show her how to incorporate the rings into her dance routine: wave them up and down and swing them from side to side.

• Play dancing music you both enjoy, and join your toddler as she swings to the beat and makes the ribbons float and twirl.

• Put the rings on the floor and dance around them, or pass the rings back and forth as you sashay past each other. Encourage her to improvise with her pretty new props.

CHILDREN LOVE THE COLOR, motion, and drama of these rippling ribbons as they spin and dance across the room.

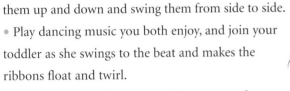

IF YOUR CHILD ENJOYS THIS ACTIVITY, also try Scarf Tricks, page 236.

285

MAGNIFY MATTERS

GETTING A BUG'S-EYE VIEW OF THE WORLD

SKILL SPOTLIGHT

Using a magnifying glass *is a superb way to help a child appreciate nature. When a leaf isn't just a leaf but a complex maze of intersecting lines, or when a tiny bug suddenly has eyes, legs, and a mouth, your toddler learns that nature is rich and complex. Helping her describe what she sees builds her vocabulary, too.*

Concept Development	✔
Language Development	✔
Size & Shape Discrimination	✔
Tactile Stimulation	✔
Visual Discrimination	✔

ENHANCE YOUR CHILD'S curiosity about her world — and her understanding of it — with a magnifying glass. She'll marvel at how grains of sand look like multicolored boulders and how flat green leaves are etched with tiny lines.

• Start your exploration by taking your child on a walk outdoors. Show her how to hold the magnifying glass up to different objects — such as leaves, rocks, grass, flowers, sand, even bugs — and look through it. Encourage her to touch the objects under scrutiny and help her find the appropriate words to describe them.

• Talk about concepts of size ("That pebble was little until we looked at it with the magnifying glass. Now it looks really big!"). Be sure to

AN ORDINARY ROCK and pinecone become intriguing landscapes of texture when your child has the chance to examine them up close and personal.

exercise extreme caution on sunny days; when the sun's rays are shining through the magnifying glass they can burn skin or even start a fire.

- Take her for a walk indoors, too. Tell her to get an up-close view of a blanket, her toast, a houseplant, her stuffed animals, or the hair on your pet. Ask her to describe what she sees, suggesting words if she doesn't have the vocabulary.

- Also use the magnifying glass to build body awareness. Let her explore her toes, fingerprints – and even your eyes and tongue.

COUNT AND SEEK

FINDING THE MATCHING OBJECTS

SKILLSPOTLIGHT

Finding the objects *will boost your child's self-esteem (so don't hide the objects too well). Counting aloud as he finds them will help him learn both the sequence of numbers and an elementary concept of addition. The challenge of finding an object that he saw just a few moments ago also helps build visual memory.*

Counting Concepts	✔
Visual Discrimination	✔
Visual Memory	✔

◀ *IF YOUR CHILD ENJOYS THIS ACTIVITY, also try Flashlight Fun, page 262.*

YOUNG CHILDREN of all ages love finding a hidden object — whether it's a baby's rattle, Mommy's face, or a cookie hidden in Daddy's pocket. Asking a child to find more than one object adds counting practice to the fun. Simply collect three or more similar items such as cups, shoes, wooden spoons, or colored balls. Show them to your toddler, hide them around the house (leaving a part of the "hidden" objects exposed so your child can find them more readily), then ask him to search for them. Count out loud and applaud every time he finds one. To make the game harder, hide more matching objects.

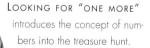

LOOKING FOR "ONE MORE" introduces the concept of numbers into the treasure hunt.

LEAF LINEUP

SORTING BY SIZE

YOUR CHILD IS QUITE INTENT on identifying his possessions ("That's my spoon!") and sorting them into various categories ("These are my hats. These are my shoes."). Take advantage of his dual love of possessions and sorting by creating a leaf collection. Gather small, medium, and large leaves. Tape one example of each size onto the sides of paper bags or small boxes. Place the rest of the leaves in a pile. Ask your child to sort the leaves into the correct bag or box according to size. While he sorts, talk to him about the leaves — where they came from, for instance, and their colors. Having a hard time finding leaves? Cut out some leaf shapes from colored construction paper.

SKILL SPOTLIGHT

Categorizing things *is immensely interesting for toddlers because it's a way of organizing and even controlling the world around them. This activity lets them learn the concepts of big and small and practice identifying which objects are which size. Talking about leaves also teaches children the words for colors and sizes and gives them a brief nature lesson.*

✔	**Classifying Skills**
✔	**Concept Development**
✔	**Language Development**
✔	**Size & Shape Discrimination**

WHAT GOES WHERE? Sorting a leaf collection is a great way to expand his understanding of big, medium, and small.

289

DUST BUSTING IS a chore toddlers adore, so let your little helper make this task more fun for you – and let her know that her work is appreciated.

RESEARCH REPORT

Many parents *are surprised at the gusto a young child will bring to everyday activities such as sweeping the floor or sponging off a counter. Yet almost a century ago, an Italian physician and educator named Maria Montessori trumpeted the value of meaningful chores – among many other revolutionary notions about early childhood. She said such chores help promote a child's sense of responsibility and self-esteem, and allow her to feel like she's contributing to the family or classroom. Today at the thousands of schools worldwide where teaching is based on Montessori's theories, classrooms are stocked with low-standing sinks, pint-size brooms and mops, and other cleaning supplies, and even the youngest preschoolers are expected to help.*

COPYCAT

IMITATING THE ADULT WORLD

SHE'S CARRYING YOUR HANDBAG and talking to the pets the same way you do. Sometimes it's delightful and sometimes it's embarrassing: do you really say, "Get down!" in that tone of voice? Now make imitation a joint activity — and get some chores done in the process.

• Encourage your child to "help" you rake leaves, dust, sweep, build a birdhouse, or fix a broken step. You can give her tot-size tools or safe adult ones, or just let her perform her tasks with make-believe supplies. She'll love giving you a helping hand.

• If you have a family pet, ask your toddler to help you feed, groom, exercise, or play with it. Not only will she learn new skills, she'll also learn to nurture the animal just as you nurture her.

• A garden is an ideal place for a child to lend a hand. Demonstrate how to plant seeds, then let her try. When the planting is long forgotten and the first shoots come up, you can surprise your young gardener by showing her the fruits of her labor.

• Adding music to your projects is a great way to enhance any task — especially if you whistle (or sing) while you work.

IF YOUR CHILD ENJOYS THIS ACTIVITY, also try Mini Mimes, page 278.

SKILLSPOTLIGHT

Children learn *by observing others – especially their parents. This wonderfully interactive activity is a good way to show your child day-to-day chores (although she's not ready to be assigned large tasks yet). It also boosts her confidence as she pretends to accomplish what Mommy and Daddy do. Imitating your voice and gestures builds auditory and visual skills; doing it to music helps her explore rhythm.*

✔	**Coordination**
✔	**Gross Motor Skills**
✔	**Listening Skills**
✔	**Role-Playing**
✔	**Social Skills**

291

GLOSSARY

ABSTRACT THOUGHT
The ability to imagine and discuss people, ideas, and objects when they are not physically present. Pretending, notions of time, finding a lost object, and making plans to visit a friend all require some degree of abstract thought.

AUDITORY DEVELOPMENT
The auditory system's maturation, which is necessary for spoken language development.

BALANCE
The ability to assume and maintain body positions against the force of gravity. A sense of balance is crucial for learning how to roll over, sit, crawl, stand, walk, and run.

BILATERAL COORDINATION
The ability to use both sides of the body simultaneously, whether or not the movements are symmetrical. A child needs bilateral coordination to crawl, walk, swim, catch, climb, and jump.

BODY AWARENESS
An understanding of what limbs, joints, and muscles feel like and the ability to locate one's body parts.

CAUSE & EFFECT
How one action affects another. Experience with cause and effect helps a child learn how her actions create a result.

CLASSIFYING SKILLS
The ability to group objects according to a common characteristic, such as size, shape, or color.

COGNITION
Mental or intellectual abilities, including the ability to solve problems and remembering routines, people, and object placement.

COGNITIVE DEVELOPMENT
A child's growing understanding and knowledge, and her developing ability to think and reason.

CONCEPT AWARENESS
An understanding of specific concepts, such as open/closed and big/little, gained through play, exploration, movement, and experience.

COORDINATION
The ability to integrate all of the senses to produce a movement response that is smooth, efficient, and skillful, such as reaching for and grasping an object.

COUNTING CONCEPTS
The ability to recite numbers in the correct order and to recognize one-to-one correspondence.

CREATIVE EXPRESSION
Using voice, movement, or art (such as painting or drawing) to communicate feelings and ideas.

CREATIVE MOVEMENT
Using bodily motion (such as imitating animals or dancing) to communicate feelings and ideas.

DENDRITES
Branching neurons that carry nerve impulses within the brain. Researchers believe mental stimulation increases the size and complexity of dendrite networks, which consequently improves cognition.

EYE-FOOT COORDINATION

Gauging distance and depth with the eyes and processing that information to coordinate when and where to place the feet. Eye-foot coordination is required, for example, when kicking a target or walking on an uneven path.

EYE-HAND COORDINATION

Directing the position and motion of the hands in response to visual information, such as reaching out and grasping an offered toy.

FINE MOTOR SKILLS

Control of the small muscles, especially those in the hands, to execute small movements, such as picking up a raisin or plucking a blade of grass. This progresses to using tools such as spoons, pencils, or scissors.

GRASP AND RELEASE

The ability to purposefully reach out and retrieve an object and let it go.

GROSS MOTOR SKILLS

Control of the large muscles, such as those in the arms and legs. Gross motor activities include crawling, walking, and running.

IMAGINATION

The ability to form mental images of what is not present. Imagination involves the act of creating new ideas by combining past experiences. It also involves abstract thought. Imagination enables a child to practice roles, predict outcomes of his behavior, and create new scenarios.

LANGUAGE DEVELOPMENT

The complex process of acquiring language skills, including understanding human speech, producing sounds and spoken language, and eventually learning how to read and write.

LISTENING SKILLS

The ability to discern various sounds, including music, rhythm, and pitch, as well as the intonations of spoken language.

LOGICAL REASONING

The ability to make decisions or take actions based on an understood progression of facts or physical characteristics. Sorting, nesting, and stacking objects all depend on logical reasoning. A toddler's understanding that she needs to drag a chair over to the desk in order to reach the computer also shows logical reasoning.

LOWER-BODY STRENGTH

The development of muscles in the legs and lower trunk, which is crucial to crawling, walking, and eventually running and climbing.

NEURONS

Long nerve cells that carry electrical impulses throughout the body. Different kinds of nerve cells enable us to move our body, think, use our senses, and experience emotions.

OBJECT PERMANENCE

The concept that an object that is no longer visible still exists.

PROBLEM SOLVING

The ability to work out a solution to a mental or physical puzzle. A child solves a problem when he figures out how to fit a piece into a puzzle, stack nesting boxes, or open a package.

REFLEXES

Automatic responses to stimuli and events (for example, putting your hand up to stop a ball from hitting you).

RHYTHM EXPLORATION

The act of exploring the rhythms and underlying beat of music through movement.

GLOSSARY

ROLE-PLAYING
Mimicking the actions of others and eventually using imagination to pretend to be someone or something else.

SELF-CONCEPT
A child's understanding that he is an individual person separate from his parents.

SENSORY EXPLORATION
Using the senses—hearing, sight, smell, taste, and touch—to learn about the world.

SHAPE RECOGNITION
The ability to identify specific forms, such as circles and triangles. Shape recognition eventually helps a child learn to read and write.

SIZE & SHAPE DISCRIMINATION
The ability to identify objects of different dimensions and their relationship to each other, such as nesting boxes or pieces in a puzzle.

SOCIAL DEVELOPMENT
A child's growing understanding of her interactions with people and her influence on her world.

SOCIAL SKILLS
Interacting and relating to other people, including recognizing other people's emotions through their tone, actions, or facial expressions.

SPATIAL AWARENESS
Knowing where one's own body is in relation to other people and objects. A child uses spatial awareness to crawl under a bed, walk between two objects, and generally move through space.

SYNAPSES
The tiny gaps between neurons through which electrical impulses jump, thus allowing nerve cells to communicate with one another.

TACTILE DISCRIMINATION
The ability to determine differences in shape or texture by touch. Being able to discern textures helps children explore and understand their environment and recognize objects.

TACTILE STIMULATION
Input to receptors that respond to pressure, temperature, and the movement of hairs on the skin. Tactile stimulation enables a child to feel comfortable with new experiences such as first foods and unexpected touch.

UPPER-BODY STRENGTH
The development of muscles in the neck, shoulders, arms, and upper trunk, which is crucial to crawling, sitting, pulling up, and walking.

VISUAL DEVELOPMENT
The maturation of a child's eyes and eyesight.

VISUAL DISCRIMINATION
The ability to focus on and distinguish objects within a visual field. A toddler uses visual discrimination to find a bird in a picture, a desired toy in a basket, or locate a parent in a crowd.

VISUAL MEMORY
The ability to recall objects, faces, and images. Visual memory allows a child to remember a sequence of objects or pictures. It also serves as a foundation for learning to read.

VISUAL TRACKING
The ability to follow the movement of an item by moving the eyes and rotating the head.

SKILLS INDEX

SKILLS INDEX

SKILLS INDEX

INDEX

 # ACKNOWLEDGMENTS

A VERY SPECIAL THANKS to all the children, parents, and grandparents featured in this book:

Tyler & Ashlynn Adams
Robin & Jessica Alvarado
Eric Anderson
José & Anna Arcellana
Lisa & Summer Atwood
Greg, Denise, & Aiden
  Ausley
Debbie & Karly Baker
Madeleine Barnum
Maiya Barsky
Leticia & Mikailah Bassard
Dana, Nicholas & Robbie
  Bisconti
Whitney Boswell
Annamaria & Sean Mireles
  Boulton
Catherine & Lizzie Boyle
Brynn & Riley Breuner
Jackson Breuner-Brooks
Danielle Bromley & Tyler
  Primas
Chizzie & Patrick Brown
Ashley Bryant
Madison Carbone
Millie Cervantes & Norma
  Foreman
Kailah Chavis
Christian Chubbs
Tami & Averie Clifton
Katherine & Parker Cobbs
Kelly, Mark, & Rebecca Cole
Jamila Coleman
Kevin & Sofia Colosimo
Kim & Katherine Daifotis

Bolaji, Kyle, & Miles Davis
Jane, Lauren, & Robert Davis
John & Jessica Davis
Keeson Davis
Justice Domingo
Elaine Doucet & Benjamin
  Martinez
Kimberly & Jacob Dreyer
Margaret & Lauren Dunlap
Stacy, Sydney, & Sophie
  Dunne
Tiffany & Simon Eng
Edgar & Melanie Estonina
Masooda & Sabrina Faizi
Christina Fallone
Kristen & Kaitlin Fenn &
  Susan Carlson
Quinn Folks
Shannon & Clayton Fritschi
Terri & Jacob Giamartino
Kristen Gilbert & Phenix
  Dewhurst
Wendi & Joshua Gilbert
Patricia & Nathan Gilmore
Galen Gold
Sharon & Annabel Gonzalez
Alexa Grau
Carrie Green-Zinn &
  Zaria Zinn
Jade & Jordan Greene
Candace Groskreutz &
  Matthew & Clare Colt
Annette, Katie, & Connor
  Hagan

Walter, Ester, & Whitney
  Hale
Danny & Yasmine Hamady
Drew Harris
Arthur & Reed Haubenstock
Ashley & Alyssa Hightower
Cameron & Bix Hirigoyen
Laurasia Holzman-Smith
Justin Hull
Margy Hutchinson & Isaiah
  Hammer
Rochelle Jackson
Ryan Jahabli-Danekas
Stephanie Joe & Alexander &
  Isabelle Weiskopf
David Johnson
Lynne Jowett & Eloise Shaw
Elana Kalish
Gilda & Megan Kan
David & Giselle Kaneda
Ashley Kang
Esther Aliah Karpilow
Isabella Kearney
Thomas Keller
Denise, Chloe, & Ian Kidder
Caecilia Kim & Addison
  Brenneman
Jeff, Jennifer, Sydney,
  & Gunner Kinsey
Sonya Kosty-Bolt & Owen
  Bolt
Dan & Martin Krause
Isabelle Jubilee Kremer
Olivier & Raphael Laude

Mark & Samantha Leeper
Mary & Simon Lindsay
Darien & Nicholas Lum
Peg Mallery & Elliot Dean
Alicia & Devon Mandell
Lily Marcheschi
Kim & Miles Martinez
Beth & Alison Mason
Lisa & Zachary Mayor
Nathaniel McCarthy
Ryan McCarty
Meredith & Sam McClintock
Susan McKeever & Sophia
  Rosney
Jennifer, Jim, & Abigail
  McManus
Alex Mellin
Maya & Jakob Michon
Sarah Miller & Elizabeth
  Schai
Justin Miloslavich
Kimberly Minasian &
  Isabelle Schulenburg
Lou, Terri, & Lou Molinaro
Mikayla Mooney
Nikolaus Moore
Theresa & Gabriel Moran
Mary, Jeff, & Amanda Rose
  Morelli
Tom, Genevieve, & Graham
  Morgan
Madeleine Myall
Chantál & Kalle Myllymäki
Betsy & Megumi Nakamura

Abby Newbold
Carly Olson
Sue, Katie, & Christine
  Partington
Terry, Kim, & Hunter
  Patterson
Elizabeth & Hayden Payne
Abigail Peach
Lori Pettegrew & Andrew Pike
Henrietta & Katie Plessas
Santiago Ponce
Bronwyn & Griffin Posynick
Jim & Kira Pusch
Shanti Rachlis
Ann Marie Ramirez &
  Damien Splan
Miles Reavis
Wayne & Thomas Riley
Kali Roberts
Aliyah Ross
Blake Rotter
Lori, Mark, & Zayle Rudiger
Renée Rylander & Ryan
  Ditmanson
Christine & Matthew Salah
Leigh & Kai Sata
Eloisa Tejero & Isabella Shin
Joseph Shin
Haley Shipway
Kathryn Siegler
Michelle Sinclair & Nicolas
  Amerkhanian
David Sparks
Colleen & Maxwell Smith

Nicole & Marlo Smith
Julia Stark
Jackie & Jaylyn Stemple
Denise & Adam Stenberg
Brisa & Diva Stevens
Quincy Stivers
JoAnne Skinner Stott &
  Sonja Stott
Lori & Karl Strand
James & Jayson Summers
Sandi, Kimberly, &
  Jacquelyn Svoboda
Michelle & Tatum Tai
Dylan Thompson
Rico & Deena Tolefree
Alisa & David Tomlinson
Kathi & Lauren Torres
Lila & April Torres
Mahsati & Kiana Tsao
Annalisa & John "Jack"
  VanAken
Paula Venables
Jim Vettel & Peyton Raab
Sebastian & Julian von Nagel
Gabriel Wanderley
Jenifer Warren & Grace
  Bailey
Patty & Shawn Weichel
Molly & Jamie Wendt
Kathleen & Meredith
  Whalen
Pernille & Sebastian
  Wilkenschildt
Daisy & Karinna Wong

Emma Wong
Sara Wong & Dean
  & Jack Fukushima
Catherine Wood
Tina & Anna Wood
Ajani Wright
Amy & Marissa Wright
Preeti & Shama Zalavadia
Allison, Jill, & Nicole Zanolli

Karen Zimmerman & Jarred
  Edgerly
Lisa Zuniga & Maria Carlsen

*Mirror on page 184 courtesy
of Mudpie in San Francisco.
Crayola and serpentine design
are registered trademarks of
Binney & Smith and are used
with permission.*